Environmental Cognizance

Towards the Year 2020

Environmental Cognizance

Towards the Year 2020

John C. Krieg

www.ivyhousebooks.com

PUBLISHED BY IVY HOUSE PUBLISHING GROUP
5122 Bur Oak Circle, Raleigh, NC 27612
United States of America
919-782-0281
www.ivyhousebooks.com

ISBN: 1-57197-436-9
Library of Congress Control Number: 2004110873

Printed in the United States of America

To the staff and students in the
horticulture/landscape architecture program at the
State University of New York at Cobleskill.
May the circle remain unbroken.

Other books by John C. Krieg

Desert Landscape Architecture, 1999
Eco Nation, coming in 2005
Funding the Green Revolution, coming in 2006

Table of Contents

Then God said, "Let the waters teem with fish and other life, and let the skies be filled with birds of every kind." So God looked at them with pleasure, and blessed them all. "Multiply and stock the oceans," he told them, and to the birds he said, "Let your numbers increase. Fill the earth!" That ended the fifth day. And God said, "Let the earth bring forth every kind of animal—cattle and reptiles and wildlife of every kind." And so it was. God made all sorts of wild animals and cattle and reptiles. And God was pleased with what he had done. Then God said, "Let us make a man—someone like ourselves, to be the master of all life upon the earth and in the skies and in the seas." So God made man like his maker. Like God did God make man; Man and maid did he make them. And God blessed them and told them, "Multiply and fill the earth and subdue it; you are masters of the fish and birds and all the animals. And look! I have given you the seed-bearing plants throughout the earth and all the fruit trees for your food. And I've given all the grass and plants to the animals for their food." Then God looked over all he had made, and it was excellent in every way. This ended the sixth day.

—Genesis 1:20–31
The Living Bible

Works Cited

1.) *Water: A Natural History.* Outwater, Alice. New York: Basic Books, 1996.

2.) *The Chaneysville Incident.* Bradley, David. New York: Harper & Row, 1981.

3.) *Nature's Keepers: On the Front Lines of the Fight to Save Wildlife in America.* Tobias, Michael. New York: John Wiley & Sons, 1998.

4.) *Use Less Stuff: Environmental Solutions for Who We Really Are.* Lilienfeld, Robert, and William Rathje. New York: Ballantine Publishing Company, 1998.

5.) *Song of the Dodo: Island Biogeography in an Age of Extinctions.* Quammen, David. New York: Touchstone, 1996.

6.) *Let the Mountains Talk, Let the Rivers Run: A Call to Those Who Would Save the Earth.* Brower, David, and Steve Chapple. Gabriola Island, BC, Canada: New Society Publishers, 2000.

7.) *The Botany of Desire: A Plant's View of the World.* Pollen, Michael. New York: Random House, 2001.

8.) *Buffalo for the Broken Heart: Restoring Life to a Black Hills Ranch.* O'Brien, Dan. New York: Random House, 2001.

9.) *Redesigning the American Dream: The Future of Housing, Work, and Family Life.* Hayden, Delores. New York: W.W. Norton & Company, 2002.

10.) *Earthscape: A Manual of Environmental Planning.* Simonds, John O. New York: McGraw-Hill, 1978.

11.) *Hard Green: Saving the Environment from the Environmentalists: A Conservative Manifesto.* Huber, Peter. New York: Basic Books, 1999.

12.) *The End of Nature.* McKibben, Bill. Anchor Books New York, 1990, 2000.

Part One:

Composed circa 1999

Chapter One

The Voices of a Nation

My name is Manuel De la Hoya. I work in Phoenix, Arizona. I'm the one the gringos speak of when they say, "We can do the job with manual labor." My ancestors were Spaniards who came to take the gold from this land. I come for the same reason. What little I make I send to my family in Mexico. My ancestors were the first to proudly ride across this land on horseback. They conquered whoever and whatever stood in their path. I slouch in the seats of decrepit pickup trucks cowering from the immigration officials. It's expensive to live in this country, but I cannot afford to return to mine. I'm the one who mows the grass, plants the annuals, and butchers the trees and shrubs—or so the gringos say. I don't care if that shrub *ever* grows back again. If it doesn't my job will be easier the next time I'm here. I get paid by the job. I must finish quickly and be off to the next one. The gringos, they say I'm uneducated, that I should take the time to learn more so that I can do things right. What I've learned from my father, that he learned from his father, is this: I must work many jobs to make enough money to feed my family. In my culture, that's what's right.

I would like to properly introduce myself. My name is Teresa Thornberry. My ancestors were among the first to settle in what was then the Commonwealth of Virginia. We acquired land and grew tobacco. Eventually, we became one of the wealthiest families in the Southeast. Being from an agrarian background, I respect the land and appreciate what it can produce. The land must work for us, and we must find ways to capitalize on its bounty. Although I myself would have no need for it, *marijuana* would be a tremendous cash crop. The fuddy-duddies who oppose it are the same people who would like to outlaw tobacco. People have a right to make their own decisions. With a change in the laws, we could be in production within six months. Heartless mercenary, you call me? I'm a businesswoman, for goodness' sake.

I'm Nick Justice. I drive a cab in New York City. I've seen all sorts of people from all walks of life. In this cab, man, I've seen it all. Yeah, like the name? I picked it. Me and the old man, we didn't get along, so I said, "To hell with you. I'll get my own name. Go to hell and thank you very much." The name is kinda catchy, and it gives the passengers a warning. Go ahead and try to put one over on me. Justice will prevail. One thing about the Big Apple—it's cold and it's hard, and there's a lot of concrete. I think the street trees give people a break. The *greenery* sort of loosens them up, reminds them of the woods or something. I like the little parks. I take my breaks in them. Some are better than others. Some are beautiful. Some are full of trash—the two-legged kind. All of the parks look okay from the windows of my cab. I mean, they look better than a bunch of run-down old buildings. I wish we had more of them to soften the place up.

Slam here. Twenty-seven years old and I've been on my own for twelve years. I exist in San Diego. I sleep and drink downtown. I get to the beaches about once a week to shower in the public restrooms. That's the main thing about maintaining your self-respect when you're homeless—being able to take a shower. They call bums "bums" because they're dirty. In most cities it's hard to find showers. No wonder people become bums. They call me Slam because I can outdrink anyone. That's what they tell me, anyways. When I'm drinking, after a while, I don't know because I'm drunk. When I'm sober I can think about what a great city this is. I mean, we got the zoo, Mission Bay, Hotel Del, the beach, Balboa Park. There's a lot of great places to go, but except for the beach, I never go anywhere. I only think of these places when I'm sober, and I'm only sober when I'm broke. It costs money to ride the bus. It takes cash to get into the best places. San Diego—a city for all the people—all the people with *money*, that is.

My name is Shadow. I'm a pickpocket. I live and work in Miami. You never see me. I rise up out of the cracks in the sidewalk. I show up where you would never expect me, and I'm gone before you notice. From what I steal, I know more about you than you will ever know about me. You're a boring, predictable bunch. You live the same life every day, travel the same routes, eat in the same restaurants. You might not like what I do, but I have to be creative, elusive, and swift. I am always *cognizant* of my surroundings. Survival of the fittest, in a civilized society, does not so much depend upon strength and aggressiveness as it does upon cunning and stealth. If the country went bankrupt, if the economy plummeted—who do you think stands a better chance of surviving? You or I?

Zachary Edwards. I run a Fortune 500 company in Chicago, the city with big shoulders. How I wish that was still true. Corporations in America have been cut off at the knees. The environmentalists want more regulations and clamor for corporate responsibility. As far as I'm concerned we've been regulated into extinction, and we're supposed to be responsible for everyone else's mess. This isn't like the old days, when a man of circumstance and purpose could rise up to be a corporate giant. Now a man can make it to middle management by his forties. Any positions of real power come later—just about when you're ready to retire. Industrialization and the corporations that drove it are what made this country great. Now all the important businesses are service businesses. Let me ask you this. Who *works* anymore? Who gets down in the trenches and produces goods? No wonder the Japanese kick our butts, and what's worse, we let them do it. I wouldn't let another car, camera, or stereo into this country until they accepted our beef and agricultural products into theirs with equal ease. There's not enough ass kicking by higher-ups on lower-downs. Without stress and tension, nothing happens—and nothing is. Through the high-rise window of my executive suite, I look out and see America rot.

My name is Terrance Whitefeather. I'm a full-blooded Sioux Indian. I live on a reservation in Nebraska, and I have no desire to leave. You hear these bad things about the reservation, and you must wonder why anyone would want to stay? This is the last of all the land that once belonged to my people. I stay because here we are still a separate nation and our leaders are *still leaders.* A great chief would never eat until all the people were fed. Your white chiefs don't even know who their people are.

My name is C. J. I'm fifteen. I'm in a gang in Compton, California. In my hood you have to be; my older brother is, my younger sister is, everyone I know is. Cops always be bustin' us for graffiti. You tellin' me Indians, prehistoric brothers, people like that didn't leave signs? You know they did. It wasn't because they were bored. It was because they wanted to mark out their *territory.* Taggin' is honest. Like old times, it's needed. A man's got to know where he's at and who his enemies are.

I'm Michael Nelson, ASLA, which stands for American Society of Landscape Architects. I hail from Boston, Massachusetts. Boston is the cultural center of America. Someone out in San Francisco might argue this, but when history, art, and culture are considered in combination with *urban atmosphere,* Boston wins, hands down. I believe in historic preservation, not only of buildings but of places also. This is not so much an issue of history, as it will repeat itself soon enough. Stay in one place long enough and, like a revolving door, it will rotate in front of your very eyes. It is more an issue of parentage. We are linked to our ancestors. I like to savor the flavor of times gone by. It lets me know where I came from and gives me a yardstick with which to measure modern times. My observation is that they did much more with a lot less that has a lasting beauty. Today's society is just plain lazy. We, as a people, are stagnant. If history is our teacher, the same thing always happens in a stagnant society. People get fed up. Then they start a revolution.

My name is Will Simpson. I'm a park ranger in Montana. I love the outdoors. I love nature. I love my job. I hate the thought of losing it. As I watch one park being shut down after another I grow more fearful that mine will be the next. Where would I go and what would I do? Just what would be the odds of my obtaining a job of a similar nature anywhere in a country where the people *allow* their leaders to compromise their national environmental treasures? I'll be flipping burgers at a McDonald's while wondering if the spirit of Teddy Roosevelt will ever ride again. Take a good look at me. I'm the last of the line, a dying breed, a vanishing species. A man who so deeply cares about nature that he devotes his whole life to it has now become expendable in America.

I'm Grover Theodis—a professional football player. Number twenty-two on the roster but number one in your hearts. You know the team's name. You see us on television every Sunday. Every Monday, Thursday, and Saturday, or so it seems to the housewives across America. During the season my environmental awareness concerns grass. I love the stuff. I love the way it looks, smells, feels, tastes, and forgives violent collisions. Astroturf is from the pit of hell spawned by greedy team owners, television stations, and quite possibly laundry detergent manufacturers. Football is a rugged sport meant to be played *outdoors* on real turf by real men. I'd give up a quarter of my salary if it could be that way again. In a career constantly threatened by injury, it doesn't help that Astroturf dramatically increases the risk factor. Let's rip the tops off of dome stadiums and put in real grass. Let's get back to what this game is about—barbaric behavior displayed under an open sky no matter what the weather. One warrior trying to pummel another into the turf.

My name is Keith Connally. I'm a small-town automobile mechanic in the hill country of Tennessee. The economy around here is depressed. The people around here can barely afford to keep their cars running, much less worry about emissions levels and government restrictions. The men in my town are more worried about keeping their families fed and paying their bills than about what might happen fifty years from now. Cars regularly come into my garage with their catalytic converters disconnected. I don't like this, but I look the other way.

Slightly better gas mileage outweighs the fear of a ticket. It's just that way around here. This is minor. In fact, I think you would be surprised just how much of an *outlaw* an otherwise honest man will become when he needs to survive.

I'm Marcus Steadman, and I'm a real estate broker from Los Angeles, California. This is still the Golden State, filled with golden opportunity. There's a lot of action, and I'm in the middle of it all. First, there's tremendous inventory owing to the burgeoning population. Secondly, there's terrific turnover driven primarily by the move-up market and couples getting divorces. Every time there's a sale within my organization, I'm into it for 4 percent. Life is good. Houses have gotten smaller, lots have gotten smaller, families have gotten smaller, mortgages have gotten bigger. It's too good to be true. There's always talk that we are running out of *renewable resources,* but we always seem to come up with something just as good. Building methods and techniques are always evolving and improving. I don't see why everyone is so worried.

My name is Keith Turner. I'm a third-year college student in the five-year bachelor's program in landscape architecture at the University of Arizona in Tucson. U of A. Go cats! *I am worried* about the future. I could give you a bunch of drivel about how concerned I am about the environment, but the truth is, I'm more concerned about a job. After five years of college, what waits for me on the outside? When I was in high school I heard so much about the nineties being the green decade it made me decide to go into a career that impacts the environment. Now I ask you, if this is the green decade, where is it? Where is the sweeping change? And where are the jobs that were supposed to come as a result of the new programs? Vice President Gore has done a lot of talking, but his boss hasn't delivered. I saw a lot of young people like myself getting in line to feed off the new gravy train, but somehow or somewhere it has run off the tracks. Now we are all in danger of starving.

My name is Monte Mindenhower. I'm a transportation engineer in Little Rock, Arkansas. America in general, especially the Deep South, is facing a transportation crisis. The country's infrastructure—her roads and bridges, her dams and reservoirs, her ports and harbors—are *falling apart.* Ross Perot made mention of this in the 1992 campaign, but it was forgotten and pushed out of everyone's minds faster than he was. The problem is very real and won't go away. I would like to return to the days of FDR. I think the government could initiate environmental and infrastructure restoration programs that would catch the attention of the population. Isn't it nice to live in a country that needs to be repaired? This should create a lot of jobs, as the task at hand is monumental. To date, nothing has happened to outline what needs to be done or to pinpoint and prioritize what can be done.

I'm a veterinarian from Sioux Falls, South Dakota. My name is Marsha Green. I've been in practice for over twenty-five years. I won't bore you with that "I'm only thirty-nine" nonsense. I have more important things on my mind than trying to impede the inevitable. America is in the midst of an *animal population explosion.* With each passing year it gets worse. Cats and dogs, especially, are getting out of control. This is particularly true in the inner cities where, like with the higher species, the overcrowding creates violent behavior. In addition, their wastes give rise to a growing sanitary problem. I know you've heard this before, but I'm going to continue to remind you until it sinks in. If you love your pets have them neutered. They cannot act responsibly, so we humans have to.

A pet without love and guidance is an animal on the verge of becoming wild and dangerous.

I hail from Seattle, Washington—a very modern city where the people are hip. My name is Patricia Powell, and I'm a right-to-life activist. This issue is so important to me that I've been forced to become a militant. I never thought I'd behave in a violent fashion, but desperate times call for desperate measures. I'll sabotage abortion clinics and intimidate pregnant women trying to use them. Some members of my ranks are in favor of killing the doctors who perform the carnage. For me, it may yet come to that. Murdering a murderer does not seem like such a bad thing to do. I support *birth control.* Rape victims can always put unwanted babies up for adoption. Why can't human beings be responsible for the consequences of their own actions? I don't like what I've become, but I can't back away now. Things may get worse in this country before they get better.

My name is Ted Greenly. I'm an Iowa farmer. I work from sunrise to sundown trying to stave off the big agricultural conglomerates who want to swallow me up. I think there is still a place for the small farmer in America, especially if he can contribute to the theory of *crop diversity*. Farms are greatly simplified ecosystems and biomes. As such, they are subject to ecological pressures. Wind, rain, drought, and climate all affect a farm. Pests and diseases are an even bigger threat. The conglomerates, with their huge acreages of the same crop, are ticking time bombs. One unstopped species of insect pests or one incurable disease could wipe out an entire year's crop. The smaller farmer, if he commits to growing different types of crops than the conglomerates, has a better chance of withstanding pestilence and infestations. By thinking in terms of crop survival under difficult circumstances he may yet ensure his own survival.

My name is Todd Burgess. I work as a plan checker for the planning department of the city of Tempe, Arizona. Most landscape architects, whose plans I review, don't like me. What they really don't like is anyone, other than a client, criticizing their work. From where I sit and from what I see, they are all pretty much the same, and there doesn't seem to be a truly original thinker in the lot of them. The municipalities and other governmental bodies are partly to blame. Their standards are mostly the same, and in defining an identifiable level of acceptance they also define the only level of acceptance. In other words, the *minimum becomes the maximum.* The second major contributor to the homogenization of the profession is the computer. Every office used to have its own system of graphic communication. Now, with less than two dozen programs available, the drawings from the firms that are on computer are all starting to look the same. Because of the limitations in the programs, some important elements of the design process are glossed over or left out. The same mistakes are made over and over again. Garbage in means garbage out. And all I'm seeing is the same old garbage day in and day out, year in and year out.

Philip Smith here. I'm a nursery man in Saint George, Utah. Man, oh man, is this area starting to grow. Business is good. The nursery business in the Southwest has changed dramatically in the last twenty years. People are demanding *native plant materials.* The concept of using site-specific plants is also gaining recognition. Devegetation/revegetation of existing trees and shrubs as well as harvesting wildflower and grass seeds to be used in the same locale from whence they came makes a lot of sense. What plants would be better suited to the area than plants that come from that area? People are becoming more biologically and environmentally aware. I'm confident that with informed and controlled growth Saint George will remain the beautiful place it now is.

Dameon Underwood's the name. Death is the game. I'm a mortician in Montgomery, Alabama. Business is steady. Americans are phobic about their dead. It's only the extreme cost of a funeral that forces them to even consider cremation. Neither what I do or the ashes-to-ashes, dust-to-dust routine does much for the environment. Has anyone ever considered *human composting?* It all sounds so morbid, but have you ever heard of bonemeal or bloodmeal? Where do you suppose these two natural soil amendments come from? It's true that soil nutrients run in cycles. It is also true that soil structure is determined by decomposed organic matter. The more organic matter and nutrients that are introduced into the soil the more friable and fertile it becomes. Why do I mention this? It's a scientific fact that all natural resources on Earth are limited in quantity and some, like fossil fuels, are nonrenewable. As the human population on Earth builds geometrically, more resources are being drawn out of the Earth than are being put back into it. The day will come when there will not be enough life-giving natural resources on Earth to support its population, and unless the most prolific biodegradable species on Earth gives back to the soil it will become depleted. Crop production will plummet, and then famine and death will ensue.

Bennie Fountnot is my name. New Orleans is my home. I love the bayou and the delta. New Orleans never sleeps, especially during Mardi Gras. In reality, there's a party going on twenty-four hours a day, 352 days a year. I'm a sanitation engineer, and down here, that's a growth industry. You've seen the news clips of the festival atmosphere, the gaiety, and the confetti. You've probably never wondered, *who cleans up*? It's me, that's who. America has a solid waste problem that stems from the disposable-container, disposable-razor, boil-in-a-disposable-bag mentality of her people. Everyone assumes that someone else will clean up. They figure someone gets paid to do it, so why worry? The truth is that our sanitation force is understaffed and underpaid. We do the best we can, but we don't get all the trash. It builds up in the back streets. It gets compressed into the nooks, crooks, and crannies. It looks like hell, but no one seems to care. The apathy gets worse at the landfills. This country has an out-of-sight, out-of-mind mentality. The problem is that the trash is building up so fast that soon it won't be out of sight. I wish everyone would take more responsibility for the amount of trash they generate, but every day I'm reminded that they don't.

People call me Stub McNeil. I'm an arboriculturist from Saint Louis, Missouri. I got the nickname Stub when I cut my ring and little finger off in a chipping machine. It's the price one pays for the work one does. In some ways it has made me more cautious when using more dangerous equipment like chainsaws and log splitters. It always reminds me to be careful in dangerous situations, such as when I'm sixty feet up in a tree. I love being in the trees. I often think that maybe the plants are God's chosen kingdom and that trees are His ultimate creations. Why else would he have made them so stately and majestic? I'm reasonably sure that they don't feel pain. I treat them with reverence. It's a privilege to work on them, cure them of pests and diseases, and somehow imagine that they could be made even more beautiful through my efforts. There's not enough trees being planted in America these days, especially in the cities. I think that Arbor Day should be a *national holiday* and that every adult American should be required to plant at least one tree on this day every year. After ten years, can you imagine what a beautiful country this would be?

I'm twelve years old. My name is Katie Williams. I live in the projects in Tampa, Florida. Every day I'm bussed to a school in a nicer neighborhood where the teachers tell us we are the future. Every night I'm bussed back to my home where I see there is no future. There's a park across the street that my friends and I *never play in.* It's full of drug dealers and drug addicts. I don't look at them. I don't want to know who they are. My father is over there, and so is one of my aunts. I don't want to ever be over there. I can't wait to grow up so I can get out of this place. Until I'm old enough to leave I wish there was a safe park around here where kids could play.

My name is Jerry Golding. I'm a real estate developer in Santa Fe, New Mexico. You've heard of the Santa Fe style of architecture. It was born by the usage of indigenous building materials—adobe blocks from clay in the soil and timbers from cottonwoods and sycamores that line the rivers and streams. The architecture arises out of the environment, and the environment is visually enhanced by the architecture. While this may not be a true symbiotic relationship, at least it's a harmonious one. Like other developers in the Southwest, I face a lot of restrictions whenever I try to build on a new piece of ground. Sometimes I feel handcuffed by the local government. About the only concern I feel I don't have an answer for is *water conservation.* The West is running out of water. While I try to make my homes as energy and water usage efficient as possible, the day will come when I will no longer be allowed to build.

These are the voices of a nation. The thoughts, opinions,

and dreams of the people of the United States. This is the country where I live and work. You have probably heard similar voices in the land that you inhabit. In their simplest forms, lying just beneath the surface of tone and dialect, they are speaking of a concern they have for the outcome of their lives. In their collective form they grow loud and restless. As individuals they are not much united on anything. As a dichotomy of a society they echo the sound of something promised but not delivered, of something needed but not seen. Like a mob outside a courthouse, their voices become boisterous and clamoring. What they want lives in their imagination, vaguely rubbing shoulders with hope and aspiration. Impatiently they wait, for soon they will not only witness but rather they will become intermixed with and an integral part of an environmental revolution.

Like all revolutions, this revolution will fall short of its loftier goals but will effect some positive change by implementing the more practical ones. There will come a recognizing of the need to be somehow attached to the Earth when we are of it. We become attached through an awareness, a cognizance that we were meant to walk upon the land and rise to the position of dominant species. But as the dominant species it becomes necessary for us to become caretakers of the others, for we have now evolved an intelligence that lets us see that in order for us to survive they must also survive.

Cognizance. To be aware. To know the lay of the land. To be able to read it and live off of it. To respect it and know when it needs to be harvested, rejuvenated, left alone. Environmental cognizance. To see the larger picture of the Earth. How oceans, continents, and atmosphere interact. Macro conditions that cause geographic and geological events. Environments—a reduction in scale. Continental impacts but not necessarily worldwide ramifications. Biome—range and definition. If this were a lens it would be in a microscope. Habitat and communities. Species and territory. Individuals within the species—you. Yes—*you.* Do you possess environmental cognizance?

Are people really cognizant of the environment, or anything else, for that matter, that's outside the realm of their immediate influence? We are territorial creatures, and that territory—that area beyond the house and car—is typically a very small place. Same job, same route, same stores, same stadiums, same restaurants. About the only time horizons are broadened are during family vacations to faraway and exotic places just strange enough to attract your relatives. No, our world is a small one—getting smaller still.

How do we connect with the Earth? How do we walk upon the land and know our place? We just do. We insist on it as a part of our internal sanity. We believe in the power of trees and never let them out of our sight. For if we do, the concrete, the steel, the lights, the pollution—visual and otherwise—will swallow us up and bury us deep within another layer of the evolutionary mantle that is the Earth's crust. All is gone of one world, and adapted man will have to somehow climb one rung higher on the evolutionary ladder to reach the next.

But the Earth, when it's peaceful, is a beautiful place. I'm in no hurry to witness the coming of adapted man while at the same time knowing that my kind will soon be forever extinct. It would be a dark, eerie time, and I thank God and truly believe that I'm on this Earth—right here, right now—for better than that.

I want the species Homo sapiens to have a long and joyous tenure on this Earth, and I want their voices to be heard.

Chapter Two

Broad Brush Strokes

Let's get out the old paintbrush, a big, sloppy, four-incher. Our paints are in wide, open-mouthed buckets. Initially, we are going to work furiously with basic colors—greens, browns, and blues—earth, soil, and water. The world is our canvas, and we are going to slap the paint on generously. Vertical strokes for longitude, horizontal for latitude—Earth's ultimate definitive lines. Where they cross represents the merging of environments, and where they touch and blend indicates subtle transitions from one specific biome to another. This is going to be fun.

Switching to a smaller and tighter canvas. International cartographer's colors. Red—cities. Yellow—cropland. Light green—cropland/deciduous forest. Dark green—coniferous forest. Dark blue—swamps. Tan for grasslands and deserts. Gray and ice blue for barren, worthless land. Water, predominately oceanic, is in white or light blue and occupies 60 percent of the planet.

Water—the great thermal regulator. With its oceanic currents, a primary intercontinental transporter. Fresh water, the essential giver of life on Earth. We're lucky to have it. The other planets in our solar system have none, and look at the amount of life they sustain. What do the colors do? They follow latitude lines in a predictable, rhythmic, tumbling fashion. Parallel environments give rise to parallel evolution. Added diversity to life on Earth.

Think of the Earth as the bubble in a carpenter's level. The line is always level and always widest at the middle—the equator. Warmest, most humid. The part of the Earth that is always closest to the Sun as it spins in its orbital track. The Earth is the ultimate planetary game show. The little spin yields night and day. The big revolution (around the Sun) takes a year. Always spinning in one direction. This constant spinning creates motion, force, turbulence. This gives rise to winds and ocean currents, all moving in a more or less predictable direction at a predictable rate of speed. These distribute thermal bands above and below the surface of the Earth.

Wind carries clouds and clouds carry moisture, and land, either by height or dryness, demands this moisture. The concept of climate is born. Because of reoccurring events, life forces—environments, biomes, communities, and species—are locked into a cycle or series of cycles. Oftentimes the stability of the cycle(s) determines the stability of the biome. Everything is dependent on a series of climatic factors and the succession of when these factors occur.

The north/south axis of the Earth, while perceived as being straight up and down, is not really perpendicular to the Sun. Add the Moon—a lesser sphere in our solar system vying for the Earth's gravitational attention. The axis is canted twenty-three and one-half degrees off of a true right angle. The orbital plane would be completely horizontal in a perfect world. But, as we all know, there is no such thing as a perfect world. The Earth wobbles as it spins much as a top does when running out of inertia. This wobbling creates sun and shadow. Summer and winter solstices. The seasons are created. Then there is some form of diversity, and life on Earth must react and adapt to this diversity.

Ecological timing. When the young are born. At what time and season? Always, invariably, inevitably, a time that assures the greatest window of survivability. God, in his wisdom, tells the creatures when to come and go and when to reproduce. Man doesn't listen.

Climate—the four seasons. Dwindling sunlight triggers photoperiodism. Birds fly south for winter. Lemmings march to the sea. Two distinctly different good-of-the-species survival strategies. Both have merit in the areas of population regulation and *carrying capacity*.

Carrying capacities of niches, habitats, biomes, environments, continents, and the Earth is what ecology is all about—achieving a balance where life processes (including death) can be accommodated and allowed to come to fruition.

Stability—when one is at home with his environment and it is looked upon as safe. It is safe because it can be expected to sustain life. And then it becomes unsafe because everybody wants it. This gives rise to wars. Man's domination over his fellow man.

National land ownership equates to Earth ownership. Maximizing the land for man's highest and best purpose. Wealth was invented and a class system instituted.

Pressures upon the land become unbearable. Again—carrying capacity. The land breaks down. Soil fertility dwindles, root systems spread less, and erosion ensues. In nature, problems build slowly, yet geometrically, and then they explode.

Nature is unforgiving, or so nomadic man thought. He rode ahead of the problems and was able to save his wildness by taking as much as he could quickly and then moving on. It wasn't a long-range plan; it was merely an existence.

European feudalism was born of the land. American sharecropping. The conglomerates pushing the small farmer out. The land and what it's capable of producing as a basis of barter for food, goods, protection.

But land is nothing without air and water. It cannot sustain life in and of itself. All three are needed to support the green plants. These are the ultimate ecological creatures. Autotrophs. Self-sustaining and recyclable, yet man credits them with no intelligence. Consider, however, that without the benefit of locomotion, with few protective devices, they have been on this planet far longer than us and will probably be around, in one form or another, long after we are gone. They have taken the largest single provider of energy, the Sun, and utilized it for food production. Their leaves purify the air, while their root systems filter the water. They occupy the bottom of the food pyramid. They are the essential fibers and strands which, when woven together, comprise the food web. In a world where we harvest, eat, burn, or otherwise destroy them, the green plants endure.

The air. The fastest natural way to die is to deprive the lungs of oxygen. Next is to go without fresh water. With the importance of these two elements so apparent, it's a mystery, a self-destructive death wish, that we pollute both with increasing regularity. Air, because of its sheer mass, dilutes pollutants. Water can do the same to a point, but because fresh water is so precious, totaling just 3 percent of the total of the Earth's surface, its value as a diluter is limited. Its turnover rate in the hydrological cycle has been altered. At current usage rates the

Earth is running out of fresh water. While many environmentalists warn of severe famine, it will be the lack of available fresh water that will signal that human life on Earth has increased beyond her means to support it.

Again—carrying capacity. This is where the Earth says enough is enough, and the humans will have to figure out a way to survive.

What signals that carrying capacities are exceeded? Resource depletion, pollution, lack of ecological diversity, starvation. Once a carrying capacity has been disrupted it will take a catastrophic event within the biome to bring it back into line.

To put things into perspective, imagine carrying capacity as your bank account. What are the ramifications when there is more out in checks than is in the account? The Earth is beyond its ecological debt ratio. It is time for adjustments before our account is closed.

The sea. Frequently touted as the Earth's last remaining frontier. Vast and seemingly limitless it isn't. It's been suggested that solid and nuclear waste could be dumped in the Mariana Trench and never be noticed. Should we believe this with outer space as an option? I opt to send our wastes into the off-planet unknown. Any type of boomerang effect could prove to be cataclysmic, but leakage from those long forgotten about but still very real nuclear depth charges seems far more likely. The populations of the Earth will demand energy—even nuclear energy. It's inevitable. The sea, however, must serve a higher purpose, for soon, very soon, 2020 soon, it will have to feed us all.

If not the sea, then the estuaries that occur where land meets water. All the Earth's spinning and rotating and enduring comes to a head at the shorelines, where all the upheaval and turbulence must be regulated and turned back by the tides. The tides bring in food and oxygen and take wastes out to sea. Rich breeding grounds for flora and fauna, the estuaries of the world have the misfortune of occurring on those parts of the Earth that man most wishes to inhabit. Pollution follows man. Man settles close to shorelines. Estuaries become polluted. The areas of the Earth most capable of supporting her population are the first to come under attack by those very populations. Irony of ironies.

Landform, physiography, continents in cross section. First north and south and then east and west. The Earth is coldest at the poles because they are the farthest from the Sun. Northern North America is cold. Southern South America is cold. The Arctic land mass misses latitude eighty degrees north, so there is nothing more than large expanses of floating surface ice. Antarctica is coldest. Its land mass does fall within latitude eighty degrees south. It rises right up from the core of the Earth. Ice here is solid to the underlying land mass. A continent arises in an area that is essentially uninhabitable. It's unpolluted, pristine, militarily strategic, and lonely. Antarctica is one of the last frontiers. But this will be a high-tech frontier, an indoor existence, a testament to one's commitment to having a place on Earth, staking a claim. East and west. Shoreline, beaches, barrier mountain ranges, deserts. Latitudes six hundred to zero—where the in crowd lives. Tropical rain forests occur at zero to two hundred. From the tropic of Cancer/tropic of Capricorn to three hundred—the world's great deserts. Slightly north or slightly south, grasslands, steppes, savannahs. Land of the ungulates. Meat and grain—the staples of human diet. Then comes the deciduous forest, then boreal forest. Tundra. Ice. Oblivion.

Altitude. What goes up must come down. Temperature

changes by three degrees for every one thousand feet of elevational distance. Tundra conditions on mountain tops. Searing heat on the floor of Death Valley, which occurs at 250 feet below sea level. Biomes in cross section occur in definite strata defined by known elevations. Desert floor, bajada, chaparral, pine forest, snow cap. The environments of the Earth occur in definite identifiable horizontal and vertical patterns.

Man was always a territorial creature. It's in his nature. At first this was beneficial, as familiarity with one's habitat increases one's chance of surviving in it. Later it becomes his undoing, as overpopulation and overcrowding give rise to increasing one's territory—often by taking another's.

Man was always an adaptable creature. He went from hunter/gatherer to farmer, to craftsman, to businessman, to swindler, to politician, to dictator with relative ease.

Man was always a warlike creature. He was given aggressiveness—a penchant for mayhem. And he was given intelligence so as to best determine when, where, and how to attack, conquer, and rule over his fellow man. Slavery was the first negative end product of too much leisure time. It compounded the inherent problems of societies gone lazy by making them lazier still. They rotted from the inside out.

Man was soon a mobile creature. Domestication of horses, the wheel, cars, boats, airplanes, spaceships. Always moving faster and farther away from the Earth because he came to the realization that the world is a very small place. National trade and international commerce ensued. All roads led to Rome. Columbus discovered America. Magellan's expedition circled the globe. The Transcontinental Railroad, the Panama Canal. The family car was born. Interstate highways, toll roads, parking meters, and traffic jams. We've moved incredibly fast in order to stand still.

Then we drifted inland. Cities sprung up along navigable rivers. “Wherever there’s a city there’s a reason,” my grade school geography teacher would say. The earliest cities were always located along rivers. Ports for shipping. Fresh water for drinking. A ready transport system to carry off wastes. Cropland infringed on grazing land. Grazing land spread to irrigated chaparral and desert. The productive, fertile soil soon became cropland. Woodland was the next to go. Then the rain forests, which are the best examples of availability and selection of vegetation seeking a vertical stratification as a means to compete for light and the room to grow.

Man keeps moving and despoiling the land as he goes. As the dominant land species he has virtually eliminated his predatory competition. Now we fight amongst ourselves.

Human life on Earth. Paradoxically, the more dominant we become, the more fragile we become. As we eliminate competitive species we also lessen diversification of species. Ecological balance is thrown out of whack.

The speed with which the Earth is changing is startling. Now 4.6 billion years old, she spent the first 4 billion years, the Precambrian era, building up a decent atmosphere and harboring the prehistoric ancestors for the majority of phyla, orders, and classes found today. The Paleozoic and Mesozoic eras were refinement periods. The ever-popular dinosaurs dominated the land and became extinct, mostly during the Mesozoic era. Then came the Cenozoic era, 65 million years young—1.5 percent of the total estimated time that the Earth has been the Earth. Man appeared sometime during the last 3 million years. We’ve been on this Earth less than one full era and have had a more profound impact than any other previous species—including the mighty dinosaurs.

Like compound interest, like geometry, our numbers are

growing faster than evolution ever allowed any prior species to accumulate. Currently there is no lack of oxygen, no temperature reverses, no Ice Age to stop us. We are in charge of the course we take. Our extinction will be at our own hands. Our survival depends on balancing our populations to a level compatible to the Earth's ability to sustain us.

It's been twenty-six years since Paul Ehrlich wrote *The Population Bomb.* The birth rate in the United States has decreased to 1.5 children per family. This was not a response to the environment but rather the legacy of a worsening economy. Two-thirds of the rest of the world's countries never knew a good economy, so it never got any worse. They breed as they always have. While they wish the world would become a better place for their children, they have no real concept of how to make it a reality. The population bomb is about to explode.

Which will destroy us first? Pollution, overpopulation, nuclear warfare, disease, famine, apathy? All are avoidable so long as there is a workable planetary plan. There isn't. It's talked about in the first world and not even worried about in the third. Nowhere is it actually implemented to make any kind of a real worldwide difference. God's one creature that is given massive quantities of intelligence spends relatively little time using it to assure the survival of his own species. Man is caught up in Earth's ever-accelerating aging process. He must promote a reversal in extinction trends or perish as past dominant species have.

Broad brush strokes. The paint completes the canvas. The Earth in microcosm. The colors of life on the only living planet we know. Broad brush strokes which define the Earth. Broad brush strokes laid down by a *human hand.* Oh, what a pleasure it would be to keep them moving fluid and pure. Broad brush strokes depicting a complex entity—the planet Earth. Broad brush strokes—to keep laying them down we must never run out of paint.

Green, brown, and blue. Earth, soil, and water. Keep refilling the buckets, for as long as we maintain these colors we will maintain human life on Earth.

Chapter Three

The Global Village

Whether or not mankind across the globe wants to be, they are connected. It all started with over ocean exploration. Erik the Red was banished from Iceland for murder in 981. Setting sail westward, he discovered and settled Greenland. His son, Leif Eriksson, sailing from his native Greenland, discovered Vinland on or about 1000. Vinland, believed to be the easternmost providence of what is now Canada, must have held no special interest above and beyond that of Greenland. Eriksson overwintered in Vinland and returned to Greenland the following spring after the ice melted. If only he could have comprehended the vastness and richness of the continent that lay beyond, European history could have been quite different and settlement patterns onto the new world would have been drastically altered. But one icy island was as good as another in those days. Life was harder, simpler, and just as dangerous back then. North America would remain undiscovered for nearly another five hundred years until Columbus landed in the Bahamas in 1492. Then the murdering would commence in earnest.

In a treaty of incredible arrogance (Treaty of Tordesillas), the Portuguese and Spanish declared a line of demarcation in the New World in 1494. Spain claimed anything it found to the west of this line, while Portugal claimed all undiscovered lands to the east. Portugal, having a more established sailing tradition, quickly made several discoveries, not the least of which was massive Brazil and productive Argentina. Spain was more inclined to overland exploration and discovered central and western South America, laying claims to Mexico, Bolivia, and Peru. Then the other European countries jumped on the bandwagon.

This thirst for new lands to discover (and conquer) quickly spread throughout the civilized European world. France claimed parts of Canada. England lorded over India, South Africa, and Australia. All of the land grabbing was fueled by Christianity. The barbaric peoples of the world had to be brought to the Lord. Their land was the price they had to pay to know the kingdom of Heaven. This was by papal decree, and little effort was made to consult the higher authority.

The great Age of Discovery originating in the fifteenth century was a period of optimism. Imagine overcrowded, overfarmed Europe. Little opportunity, disease, famine, and military conscription to support kings and queens who could not care less about their people. Imagine now tales of a New World rich in food, minerals, and a chance at individual freedom. They got on the boats and took their chances.

Setting sail with crude navigational instruments and maps that were cruder still, the fear of failure and imprisonment drove them farther and farther out to sea. Antarctica, the suspected lost continent to the south, was discovered by Captain

James Cook in 1772. He returned in 1774. A glutton for punishment, maybe, but equally outlandish—perhaps he thought he could circumnavigate the globe in a north-south direction. The great Age of Discovery died with Cook—all seven continents had been located.

Considering that man appeared on the evolutionary scene about 2.5 million years ago and the last continent was discovered slightly over 300 years ago, one can see that the Earth, as humans know it, is a relatively new place.

Also, consider the theory of geometric growth, where numbers or units compound rather than build linearly. Human knowledge got a real boost during the Renaissance, which is generally credited as having begun in the fourteenth century. Then came the Agricultural and the Industrial Revolutions. Motor transport by land, sea, and air. Travel time cut to days instead of years. The rate of speed at which the Earth was discovered, overpopulated, and despoiled is alarming.

With computers, the Internet, and cyberspace, we can contact anyone in the world (who is civilized) instantly. The information highway spans the globe. You can ship packages overnight to anywhere in the world. Why then don't the people of the world know and understand each other better? They don't want to. It's like living in a small town with everyone yapping and gossiping—you steer clear of them all.

Yes, the world has made startling technological advances, particularly in the last fifty years. And then again, it hasn't. While the U.S., Canada, Russia, Australia, the European countries, and Argentina boast of a 100 percent literacy rate, Brazil is 40 percent illiterate and India and several South African countries approach 70 percent illiteracy. China and northern Africa—80 percent. The rest of the world is clueless. There are more people in the world that can't read than can.

Discussions of population control, environmental concerns, and the cooperation of governments falls on deaf ears.

But the fact remains the Earth is connected. Credit the first explorers, who bravely believed it was round because they had seen horizon lines and crossed them and then seen them again.

Winds, ocean currents, salmon swimming to their spawning grounds upstream. International shipping, intercontinental flight, worldwide telephone communications. The world is getting smaller as the information highway adds on a new lane. The problem is that half the world still lives down a dirt road.

No nation on Earth or the people it contains can shield themselves from intercontinental calamities. No one anywhere in the world truly exists in a void. We are all part of the global village, and if we're not careful there's going to be a run on the grocery store, a run on the bank, a shortage of electricity, and no running water.

It's a small town all right, and when push comes to shove we all better hope that our neighbors are friendly. If history is any indicator, however, we know that they aren't. Wars get bigger and weapons more lethal. The attitude persists—"If they get me, then I'm taking them with me." Brilliant deductive reasoning maintained and promoted by the most powerful leaders on Earth. No wonder Russia collapsed. No wonder American politicians are targets of severe lampooning in newspapers across the land.

The countries of the world are like the towns lining the interstate in rural Montana. They all like to think that they're self-sustaining, but logistically, they aren't. The highway, the thread of life that runs through them all, weaves them together. Globally, the countries of the world are connected by tides, currents, trade winds, migrations, and rain. Continentally, nations merge through roads, rails, and rivers. Unfortunately, the one thing that connects us all is intercontinental nuclear missiles. This is not what the phone company meant when it coined the phrase "Reach out and touch someone."

If physical boundaries once separated the peoples of the world, then intellectual advances have torn down the barriers. The written word, books, movies, and later the great global equalizer—television. Now human frailties threaten to throw up a wall higher than any mountain, lower than any valley, and wider than any sea. Which race is smarter? Who discovered what first? Who will take the credit? And, of utmost importance—where can we place the blame?

The scientific community is a guarded, paranoid grouping of intellectuals. High on research, low on action. Leadership is not the forte of the brilliant. It falls on those that sort of understand the breadth of the problem, those idealistic enough to believe that a solution is possible and positive enough not to look for all the reasons that one isn't. That would be you and me. The worker bees of the world must save the hive, and winter is coming. The hard-line environmentalists, biologists, zoologists, and historians all echo the same theme. The grain in the hourglass is running out. Something must be done to save the planet, but nobody seems to agree on what.

Population control is easy enough to target as a planetary environmental goal. Kicking our addiction to fossil fuels should be a worldwide goal by 2020. An international program of planting evergreen trees for the sole purpose of year-round air filtration should be mandated by governments. Water conservation is essential. Desalination of sea water, while currently cost prohibitive, will become an achievable pursuit, for when you have to have it—you have to have it. A program for urban composting of green and vegetable matter assures a steady stream of recyclable soil nutrients to the outlying agricultural areas. Recycling human excretory wastes similar to the city of Milwaukee's "Milorganite" program can put back what we take from the soil. Sustainable cities take pressure off the countryside, allowing these lands to become the transitional zones between densely populated and sparsely populated habitat areas. Then comes useable national parks, which will be appreciated more for their extreme physical beauty instead of as holding areas for a population trying but unable to escape from each other. Next, the truly wild places—grasslands, mountains, forests, and oceans.

Urban and regional planners propose that the majority of environmental problems are really issues of poor forethought and unimaginative siting of facilities and circulation systems. Levittown, Pennsylvania and Reston, Virginia are fine examples of the built environment being expertly fitted into the natural environment, but they both face issues of pollution and sanitation just like their ugly unplanned counterparts do. Paolo Soleri of the Cosanti Foundation proposes a greenhouse city under glass, but it repels the real environment on its exterior and tries to reorder and shape a new environment on its interior. This is not a policy of coexistence but rather one of avoidance. His model for the city of the brave new world—Arcosanti—sits 80 percent unfinished in Cordes Junction, Arizona, a monument to disbelieve in anything not readily achievable. Most of the new planned communities strive for diversification with schools, parks, and entertainment facilities. They usually keep the faith through the first phase, but inevitably they become what they never wanted to be—cosmetic suburbs.

Somehow, somewhere, something has to give in the area of sustainable homes, cities, regions, countries, and continents. A realistic, believable example of a man/nature/Earth interrelationship must present itself.

The global village has to see the concept of taking from the Earth and putting back, recycling if you will, in action. To promote sustainable environments which in composite lead to a sustainable Earth, the earth/life/environmental sciences have to promote positive action. Most likely it will occur in the academic community, for there must be dreamers before dreams can come true. The global village needs models to observe. The size of the model is not so much an important factor as the attention to detail inherent in its scale. A completely self-sufficient community, even of only twenty people, while small and seemingly insignificant, is just what the world has been waiting for.

With these smaller-scale models to observe, acreages of increasing size can be established, reclaimed, and preserved in their urban, semi-natural, or wild states. The problem is that land does not belong to us all or, more problematic still, that we take no pride or interest in that which we don't own. We cannot finish that which we don't start. Someone has to assume a position of leadership. The efforts of the United States-based Nature Conservancy are exemplary. This organization buys up land around the world and sets it aside for the enjoyment of all—plants, animals, and humans. They are not antidevelopment but, rather, anti careless, thoughtless development. They feel that on some levels man and nature can coexist, sometimes even in a quasi-symbiotic partnership where both entities benefit. This is the reachable middle ground in the environmental debate that rages over natural rights, animal rights, human rights, and divine rights. Any action, no matter how small, is better than no action; whether it's right or wrong or indifferent, there are precious few natural frontiers left to discover and exploit. So, we will have to make due with what we have. And then we will have to give up that which we have but don't need.

Upkeep of the global village requires an active sewer department, sanitation department, and water department. We need to elect a mayor and a chief of police. No one wants either office, for the scope of the problem far exceeds what the world is willing to pay to get it under control and hold it at manageable levels. Like the United Nations, which was established to keep world peace on a political level, an international environmental agency is needed to establish ecopolicy on a survival level. Someone, anyone, has to sound the alarm. A wake-up call to nonviolent arms is sorely needed. The scientific community, the development community, and the civilized peoples of the world all see that the day is near when the global village will be forced to get its environmental house in order. But, as they so often say—not today.

Chapter Four

Doing the Math

Ecological awareness is not so much an appreciation of beauty, as it once was, but more a need to know more in order to keep human life on Earth. In order to survive on this Earth, we must understand it. As ecological imbalance accelerates the aging process of the organisms, including man, we will have to strategize on how to maintain our position in a less diverse, less environmentally tolerant, and more competitive world. Adapted man will be a more aggressive species than sapiens. Instead of becoming a kinder, gentler place, quite the contrary, the Earth will see brutality, war, genocide, and the opening of the final chapter of the Bible in the book of Revelation. Another century older and another step closer to extinction, adapted man, our successor, may well be the last in the line of evolutionary men. The Earth may well be rid of us, and suspicions are that we will not be missed.

Could it be that mankind was an evolutionary glitch? That once corrected by elimination of the premier species (that was self-destructive, anyways), the Earth will be a better and a safer place? God would still be in his Heaven and all would still be right with what's left of the world.

We, as a species, have historically destroyed everything in our path. The despoliation of the North American continent is a particularly sad story. Alice Outwater, in her marvelous book *Water: A Natural History,* tells of how the forests were dismantled, the grasslands farmed, and our rivers and waterways dredged. She identifies four essential animal species that had an immense impact upon their habitat: the beaver, the buffalo, the prairie dog, and the alligator. The former two were trapped and hunted into near oblivion and the latter two poisoned and scorned as nuisances. Greed and ignorance reigned supreme in the initial settlement of the country, and things have not changed much since.

The beaver—cute, adorable, and industrious—created biologically diverse watersheds and wetlands. Pond sedimentation gave way to meadows and meadows to woodlands. Their dams slowed the surface flow of fresh water to its ultimate destination, the sea, and in so doing slowed the hydrological cycle to the benefit of land-dwelling organisms. Remember that fresh water is the basis of all life on Earth, as even oceanic organisms convert salt to fresh water in their internal organs. Fresh water represents just 3 percent of all water on the planet. It's something that should be kept around as long as possible.

The beaver did this by the tens of millions until their houses were ripped apart and the adults and cubs clubbed to death. As they became more wary, traps were used. They were persecuted with a relentless maliciousness into near extinction for the value of a fur coat and for the worth of an agricultural field that would quickly be made worthless as soil was depleted and not replenished. Barely a notch above the mentality of the third-world slash-and-burn countries, America exhausted her soils as her people spread west planting, depleting, and not restoring the Earth as they went.

The buffalo was the next target of unrestrained ecological mercenaries. Entire herds were slaughtered without even enough forethought to leave a few cows and calves to plunder the next year. Tongues were cut out, hides garnered, and the carcasses left rotting on the plains. The meat, which was the lifeblood of the plains Indians, decomposed in the midday sun and signaled the decay of a culture whose extinction was not far behind. Consider the advantages of buffalo over cattle, which was to become its ill-adapted replacement. The buffalo were thick chested with a massive head capable of breaking through snow and ice to underlying forage. A front mantle of dense curly hide was impervious to the blistering cold wind. These coats which kept gentlemen in the East warm were not possessed by cattle, who froze solid during winters on the prairies. The creature most suited for survival in its indigenous environment was wiped out in favor of a creature that had to be fed and protected in the dead of winter, while their owners could barely do that for themselves.

The buffalo, being wild, went to the waterways single file, Indian style, and left the same way. Cattle, being gregarious domesticates, trampled up to stream beds and ponds in mass and left dung-clogged and urine-eroded shorelines in their wake. Buffalo, in an attempt to quell flies, created wallows. These depressions in the Earth's surface eventually (when it rained) filled with mud which, when dried, protected the buffalo's hind quarters from insect bites. The wallows also acted as vertical conductors for underlying groundwater recharge. These passageways were kept open by hooves and were rapidly closed by rifles which took the hooves away. Wallows, the characteristic pocked landscape of the prairies, laid fallow and eventually filled. What looked like prime agricultural land contributed to the dust bowl of 1935, as subsurface water retreated deeper into the Earth's substrate with no natural or manmade recharge methods to keep soil saturated and cohesive near its surface.

Prairie dogs were ridiculed as competitors with cattle for the most prime grassland. Little did anyone realize that they were, in fact, the *creators* of those coveted fields. Their tunnels gave rainwater a pathway to deeper soil layers where the forces of evaporation were less demanding. The soil they dug to the surface as they created innumerable burrows was moist and rich, made richer still as it was constantly fertilized with the wastes of these energetic little rodents. What they had needed to be taken, and it was. Again, soil depletion soon followed as the takers had no notion of the biological dynamic necessary in order to give back to the land.

As the nation expanded west it also headed south, which leads us to the alligator. An ugly reptile. Toothy, single minded, and fearsome. Having few natural enemies, it was not prepared for man—soft fleshed, intelligent, and equally single minded. What the alligator showed as contempt was met with destruction of habitat which, in and of itself, caused the gator population to decline. Couple that with a tasty tail and snazzy boots, and poisoning and hunting further diminished their numbers.

Alligators have lungs and cannot live indefinitely underwater. They therefore build huge earthen mounds to lie upon and rear their young within. These mounds become staging areas for dry land plants and the myriad of other organisms that depend upon them. In addition, alligators are cumbersome creatures—they need their space. This they create by ripping out vegetation, thus creating shore-edge holes to overwinter in and open-water areas in which to swim. These areas create niches which further species diversification, which always improves ecological balance.

Man despises balance; he wants to be dominant. He doesn't do the math—so many of these plants feed so many of these creatures and create habitats for so many of these species. The only numbers that mean anything to him are zero and one. I will hunt, trap, pillage, poison, and plunder any animal outside my species for I am number one and I don't have to stop killing anything beneath me until they are no more (zero).

Eradication may prove who is dominant, but it also forever changes the face of the planet. In other words, sometimes we cut off our noses to spite our faces.

Let's, because of its dedication and beauty, listen to Outwater's impassioned plea at the end of *Water*:

> *There is the will to restore our land. We have just forgotten much of what is missing from it. The balance of nature that existed before we turned things upside down, and the richness and abundance of the land, were based on a few keystone species. What really matters are the numbers. In an area of 2.9 million square miles, billions of prairie dog tunnels and countless millions of beaver dams and buffalo wallows are significant. With their removal went an ecological system that cleaned the water and enriched the land. In spite of our earnest engineering efforts, about a third of the waterways are still polluted, and the natural water cycle is still hugely simplified. But some of the filtering mollusks and the buffalo are coming back, and the prairie dogs and the beavers have both survived with their culture intact.*

> *This land once had clouds of birds, dense herds of grazers, myriad shoals of anadromous fish—and so it could again. It is time to restore the balance to our land and allow nature's engineers to do their work. If the prairie dogs and the beavers are allowed to reestablish their ancestral populations on public land, the dirt will fly, and the waterways will begin to regain their former pristine glory. On public land, at least, it is time for the beavers and the prairie dogs to come home.* [1]

Unfortunately, the nations and peoples of the world feel that the Earth is their house and they will decide who gets to stay and who must go.

Who are the future fauna killers? How many threatened species are there? France, for such a medium-sized country, must be working overtime, as it tops the list in all five categories: mammals, birds, reptiles, amphibians, and fishes. Ever competitive, the U.S. runs a close second, while Australia, the land down under, is nip and tuck with its northern hemisphere neighbors. France is particularly tough on mammal species (59) and gluttonous with birds (132). The U.S., likewise, persecutes mammals (49) and fish species (64). Australia's mammals (45) are constantly threatened and surprisingly, so too are its reptiles (20). I guess this is because Crocodile Dundee has now taken up permanent residence in Hollywood.

Forget what is going, and let's look at what is already gone. What continents have the largest attrition rates of birds and mammals due to extinction? Judges—the envelopes please. And the winner is (mostly because of the contributions of the Americans), North America! Since 1600, twenty-two mammals and eight birds have gone the way of the dinosaur on the North American continent. Australia has killed as many mammals (22) but is lenient with its bird species (0). Asia picks up where the Aussies failed by annihilating forever and ever six bird species and a modest eleven mammals. Worldwide, seventy-three mammals and sixteen birds have disappeared since the Mayflower landed on Plymouth rock.

"Well, they probably reared up and charged," you're probably thinking. Probably so. Birds, in particular, are prone to this tact. The nonviolent plants, on the other hand, have probably fared much better. Not even. Starting one hundred years later (1700), records of threatened plant species indicate that the Australians don't like chlorophyll either, to the tune of twenty-five thousand species. The U.S. tallies twenty thousand. An unexpected entry, South Africa, being 80 percent smaller than either of the above participants, must assuredly rate as the land of the world's worst horticulturists, having obliterated twenty-three thousand species. Worldwide, the known total is one quarter million (250,000) threatened species. So much for a nonviolent existence.

Thank you contestants, one and all, for having played Wipe Out, and remember—once you kill a prize, it's yours to keep.

Surely, there must be some good news to mix in with all of this bombast. Surely, there must be a cloud with a silver lining. Well, there is. And there isn't.

Let's look at how the environmentally sensitive nations of the world have joined together in a spirit of mutual cooperation. It's easy enough to do if you count up the multilateral conventions concerning the environment. These are those convivial events where vice presidents, ambassadors, and other powerless figureheads of nations get together for photo ops, fun, and diplomacy. The host nation gains worldwide recognition as a forward-thinking government, while the host city gets a real boost to its economy, especially in the areas of alcohol sales and prostitution.

The first such event took place in London in 1933. It carried a responsible enough title as, "Preservation of Fauna and Flora in Its Natural State." Either much or little was accomplished, because the nations of the world saw no need for another such get-together until 1946 when, in Washington, D.C., "Regulations on Whaling" were enacted.

Then the ball really got rolling, first uphill and then down. The fifties saw six meetings. The sixties, eight. The seventies, especially the mid to latter parts, saw a whopping twenty-eight. Things trailed off a bit (32 percent) in the eighties, with nineteen meetings, and perhaps the backlash of this obvious sign of declining world interest was the advent and dawn of the Green Decade.

Legends, titles, nicknames, and reputations are earned and not freely given. The Green Decade has gone over like a lead balloon. To date, January 1999, there have been five international environmental conferences—five. The repressive fifties had more. The "Biological Diversity" or commonly called "Earth Summit" meeting held in Rio de Janeiro in June of 1992, for reasons to be explained in a later chapter, proved to be an abysmal failure. One has to wonder just where has the momentum of the seventies gone? Did environmentalism die with disco?

Well, there's always conservation areas. Those undisturbed acres and hectares (2.471 acres) across the Earth's surface that, because of their unique physical beauty and/or biological diversity, are set aside for the use, observation, and enjoyment of current and future generations. The Canadians, always so practical, always so woodsy, top the list with 119,478 square miles of protected lands. In an astonishing reversal of fortune, perhaps fueled by guilt, the Australians have set aside 106,363 square miles, or 3.5 percent of the continent. The U.S.—78,095 square miles, although it should be noted that the Americans differentiate between protected and public lands, of which there is an additional 7.5 million (yes million) square miles.

Great Britain (13,708 square miles) and Norway (7,272 square miles) round out the top five. Worldwide, protected areas and national parks total 1,193,618 square miles. Considering that there are 52,093,527 square miles of habitable land in the world (discounting the Arctic, Antarctic, and most of Greenland), this is a very unimpressive offering to future generations. Taking into account those nations not reporting, most notably Africa and South America, it's doubtful that the number of set-aside square miles of protected lands would double. But let's, for the sake of argument, say that they did, and we'll throw in a few hundred thousand bonus acres for good measure to arrive at a figure of 3,500,000 square miles. That's slightly less than 7 percent of all the habitable land on Earth set aside for the various publics at large and for the preservation and protection of the lower species. So much for worldwide intra/interspecies generosity. Of course, there's always Antarctica.

Land that is not set aside and not readily usable is comprised of urban deserts, mountain ranges, and grasslands. The grasslands, because of inherent soil fertility and ease of tilling, are the most quickly converted to agricultural uses. Roughly 18 percent of the Earth's habitable land surface area is grassland, and an additional 8 percent is grassland converted to prime agricultural land. Thus, 26 percent of the habitable area on Earth feeds the predominance of the population. In terms of sheer survivability, these are the areas that need protection and restoration the most. It's one thing to worry about biological diversity, and it's quite another to be around in order to have anything to worry about at all. If we can't eat, we don't live. Overworking and overgrazing are imparting huge stresses on the breadbaskets of the world. While not frequently looked upon or written about as an environmental issue, this should be the first environmental wake-up call to start the new millennium.

If we don't destroy our food sources, as expected, by 2050, are we capable of destroying ourselves from within? Yes. HIV (AIDS) statistics are changing faster than the numbers of hamburgers sold at McDonald's. The southern hemisphere is the hardest hit, especially the African continent, where the outbreak got started. There, 11 million are infected, and worse news yet, the brood stock (women) carry the larger percentage of the virus. South America, 2 million, and Australia a relatively low 25,000 plus. India and China share 3.5 million, while western Europe, usually first in all calamities large or small, tallies a very responsible 600,000. Across the Atlantic, the United States reports 1.1 million with males, by and large, most frequently afflicted. This totals 18,225,000 known cases, so let's round up to 20 million. Assuming 6 billion to be the world's total current population (on the low end), then a mere .5 percent of the world's total population is infected. Remember, and this is crucial, that a billion is *one thousand million* and not the commonly mistaken one hundred million. This should put to rest all those doomsayers who say the disease will devastate the planet. Well, maybe not. Remember that populations build geometrically and not arithmetically and so too do the diseases that those populations carry, especially if you factor in that any given carrier could have up to ten sexual partners a year. 1990 levels of 20 million could be

100 million by the end of 2000. Then, at the start of the new millennium the numbers could skyrocket. The Earth could conceivably top the billion barrier by 2006 and obliterate 12 billion by 2010. This exponential compounding of numbers kind of makes you wish you forgot about closing your first bank account. Okay, let's say it takes twice (2020) or even three times (2030) as long. There is a clear and present danger, make no mistake about it.

Or perhaps instead of fornicating ourselves into extinction we might chemically induce an unexpected subtle worldwide genocide. Again, Alice Outwater from *Water*:

> *Some of the new chemicals released to the environment have been found to interact with the body's receptors for estrogen, which appear to be not so good at recognizing what is a hormone and what is not a hormone. Nonoxylphenol polyethoxylates, used as surfactants in dishwashing liquids and toiletries, are estrogen mimics. Polycarbonate plastic, widely used in household containers and appliances, sheds bisphenol-A , an estrogen mimic so potent that 2 to 5 parts per billion are enough to induce increased hormone responses in reptiles, fish, shellfish, birds, and mammals. Endosulfan—one of the most widely used pesticides—acts like estrogen, and even the trace quantities left as residue on fruits and vegetables is enough to affect hormonal activity in many species, including human beings. DDT, PCBs, dioxins, atrazine, and some forty other compounds (many of them common household chemicals) have all been identified as hormone influences. Although these chemicals do not increase the levels of estrogen in an individual, the body perceives increased hormone levels. It is not clear how females are affected, but males of numerous animal species, from panthers to alligators, were*

> *found to have reduced sperm counts and smaller testes as a result of exposure to these chemicals, and some male fish develop genitals of both sexes. Worldwide, human sperm counts have dropped significantly since the 1940s, and a growing number of biologists believe that this may be due to environmental exposure to chemical estrogen mimics.* [1]

So much for better living through chemistry.

And then there is the issue of world health, which is probably the most real short-term threat. There is a lack of personal hygiene, particularly in the areas of inadequate or no sanitary sewer systems and nonpotable to partially potable fresh water drinking systems. Here in America, primarily due to the passage of the Clean Water Act (1972), we live in the land of plenty and don't even know it. What we take for granted is sorely missing in the rest of the world. Slightly less than 4 billion (that's billion) of the current world population is infected with intestinal parasites causing severe illness in one half billion. Deaths total in the low millions. Three parasites, the most well known being hookworm, kill over 200,000 on the African continent annually.

In an irony of ironies, wouldn't it be extraordinary to find that mankind didn't breed itself to death after all but vanished from the planet because of its inability to recognize and control attacks from chemicals and creatures predominately of its own making?

Or perhaps, in a paradox of need versus outcome, we can literally cook ourselves to death due to global warming. The automobile contributes carbon monoxide, while the cutting of old-growth temperate and tropical rain forests destroys the best users of carbon dioxide. Airborne carbon, whether mono or di, is the enemy. It bounces off the interior of the Earth's atmosphere the way a pinball bounces off of a bumper cushion. More carbon in the air holds the infrared rays of the Sun in the atmosphere for periods of increasing duration, and global warming ensues. Besides the obvious habitat destruction, deforestation represents to the lower species its biggest problem, again from a human survivability standpoint—removal of efficient processors of airborne carbon. Undaunted by the obvious, mankind will have demolished 49,540,000 acres (77,406 square miles) of old-growth woodland and 56,000,000 acres (87,500 square miles) of tropical rain forests by the year 2000. At current cutting rates, *all* of the established forest regions in the world will be required to start over by 2020.

Not that starting over, in and of itself, is such a bad thing; it's just the quality of the new timber and the lack of what it does will adversely affect the biosphere. A world full of new-growth timber will also contain four times less current biomass (leaf area and forest floor detritus) or conversely, the Earth's atmosphere will contain four times more airborne carbon than it currently does. The issue of global deforestation is certainly heating up.

Man, for the most part, is very short sighted. He tends to live for today and cross those bridges that tomorrow represents when he comes to them. Statistics usually only have meaning when applied to athletic performances or sporting events. We do the minor math in our checkbooks on a daily basis and the catastrophic math every April 14. When it comes to the environment, seldom do we know what the numbers really mean. And there's something about numbers that makes us view them as cold and unrelenting. Numbers and math are conventions created by man to keep track of wealth or systematically reproduce the same products over and over again. The science of numerology lacks vision and doesn't have a heart. It doesn't take into account man's one unexplainable attribute—compassion. No one can tell externally what is internally in a man's heart. Sometimes we amaze ourselves because, no matter how many times we crunch the numbers and do the dreadful math, the numbers just don't add up.

Somehow, some way, we will maintain our status here on Earth. This is something every decent, honest, hard-working, and compassionate human being can count on.

Chapter Five

The Value of Life

There was a welcome summer shower that blew onto the high desert plateau in late July. The sound of raindrops on the roof becomes particularly cherished in a region where they are seldom ever heard. It was 5:30 A.M., and I was on my way to work. I wasn't even speeding. As a matter of fact, I was more than five miles per hour under the limit, doing less than fifty miles per hour when it happened.

I was traveling uphill out of the chaparral-type plant community and into ponderosa pine forested mountain terrain. As I was coming around a curve, dead in front of me, smack-dab in the middle of the road, was a small animal. The road was too wet, and to try to swerve meant chancing a life-threatening accident. Briefly I hoped that perhaps it was a log. It was odd shaped and vertical in appearance, and I couldn't imagine what it was. Then it turned its head. A marble-round brown eye was encircled by a soft cream outline the size of a large doughnut. I barely felt contact. It was like hitting a pillow. Instantly I knew. A barn owl. Beautiful, majestic creatures.

There were a lot of them in the area. Immediately the rationalization process kicked in. "Well, it's not like they're an endangered species," I thought to myself. But that's not how I felt deep-down inside. There, in the place where honesty lives in all of us, I felt awful.

It was pointless to turn around, as I knew that the creature was dead. There wasn't a pullout for another three miles, and when I used it I did so to make sure that parts of the animal weren't stuck in the grill or under the frame. I felt cold and aloof and more than a little guilty, not so much for hitting the owl but for the ease with which I was putting the whole experience out of my mind and behind me. In American Indian culture it is believed that the owl is a warning sign of impending danger. I, however, subscribe to the doctrines of Christianity.

This brought me to a memory of a conversation I had had with a fellow Christian about four years prior. I was going to church regularly and even to Bible study on Wednesday nights. I was fulfilling a lifetime commitment to read the Bible in its entirety and had just waded through the Old Testament. I commented to my friend that I found it to be a disturbing piece of literature. Besides the bloody battles which were rife with human carnage, I found the sacrifice of animals particularly repugnant. My friend was not at all bothered by this. He explained that when Jesus came to Earth there was a new deal as far as animal sacrifice was concerned. This didn't do much for me, but he sloughed off my concerns by stating, "God obviously feels differently about people than he does about animals."

Six years ago I was traveling around the Salton Sea with my adoptive parents. My uncle, used to seeing baled hay garnered on the rolling hillsides of western New York, marveled at the railroad-car-size bales stacked high across the Imperial Valley. Then in Niland we drove through miles of stockyards filled with dirty cattle in wet, filthy pens, gorging themselves at the trough in anticipation of their impending death. It didn't seem like much of a life, and internally, it haunted me. I discussed this with my aunt, who explained that God had put the cattle on Earth so that man could prosper and that these doomed creatures served a higher purpose. It was reassuring news, especially since we were planning to cook rib eye steaks out on the grill for dinner that night. I know beef comes from cows, and it doesn't bother me so much except there's a feeling deep inside of me that believes that any creature that has lived a peaceful life should be allowed to walk across green grass before it dies.

But this wouldn't be practical, economically viable, or necessarily even desirable. Heavy, efficient production is what is needed to feed the hungry world. Somewhere between the demand and the production to meet the demand, the value of life got diminished.

Aside from interspecies exploitation, what does man feel towards his fellow man? If history is any indicator, open hostility, the need for complete domination, slavery, human sacrifice. As a species, we're quite aggressive. The trouble with this aggressiveness is intelligence—it enables one tribe to plot another's demise.

The external value of life is measured against the internal quality of life. If we conquer them then we will gain this. And this is where the trouble always starts. Energy transference in the ecosystem. Life must take life in order to sustain a better life. A subtle cycle of birthing and killing. A delicate balance. A dangerous line when crossed. Plant deaths replenish the soil, and animal deaths allow the younger and stronger of the species to survive and evolve. It's this slow, constant, evolving process that assures the survival of the species.

Man ignores what goes on in the natural world. He's too caught up in creating his own empires. Slavery has been with us since the dawn of civilization. The Bible is filled with accounts of it, possibly preoccupied with it in the book of Exodus. Written somewhere around 1600 B.C., it's a dreadful account of how the Egyptians persecuted God's chosen people, the Jews. They came up from Egypt to have a golden age with great leaders like David and Solomon, but they were soon after (in historical terms) conquered, first by the Assyrians and later by the Romans. By the time Christ appeared on the scene they were a dominated people in a second-rate state far from Rome and easily forgotten about. Christ, after a brief thirty-three years, was disposed of, but the legacy of his teachings flourished and lived on. These provided the social commentary whereby it was generally believed that we would all love one another. But we didn't. Slavery was rampant during the years of the Roman Empire. It barely missed a beat after the fall. And while the church denounced the practice, it recognized one that was even worse.

Feudalism supported a caste system, and while there was an avenue to rise up in the working class from apprentice to journeyman to craftsman, there was no way to become knight, bishop, king, or queen. Pawns were essentially no different than slaves, and their social status changed little until America was discovered. Those that could left their homelands and set sail for the New World. When they got there they discovered that work on one continent was no different than work on another, especially in the South. Then they turned to what they never themselves wanted to be as a solution to their problems.

Black people from the recently discovered western regions

of the African continent were unwillingly ripped from their homelands to support white people who had voluntarily left theirs. Writes noted black author David Bradley in *The Chaneysville Incident:*

> *In the year of our Lord 1441, a Portuguese sailing captain named Antam Goncalvez permitted a certain light-skinned Moorish gentleman, who was then enjoying the captain's hospitality, to ransom himself and two young male companions at the expense of ten dark-skinned gentlemen and gentlewomen from the sub-Sahara. This incident marks the beginning of the phenomenon known as the African Slave Trade.*
>
> *In recent years the study of the Trade has become something of a* cause célèbre, *for a perusal of its grim details offers white historians a gold-plated opportunity to prove their liberality and objectivity and at the same time offers black historians—the few who can get jobs—a chance to escape the paternalistic scrutiny of senior faculty members who do not quite believe that the darkies can say anything useful about anything that does not concern darkies. And so we know a great deal—perhaps too much—about the ins and outs of the Slave Trade; any historian worth his research assistant can shock the joviality right out of a cocktail party by saying that yes, between 10 and 12 million Africans were brought to the New World between 1510 and 1865 (a small matter of a fifth of the Christian calendar) and that while losses sustained during the Middle Passage were much lower than is commonly believed (a mere 13 percent to 19 percent), those incurred during the capture, the march to the coast, and the sojourn in the "barracoons" (hence the term "coon") awaiting transport were substantial enough to raise overall mortality to*

between 30.4 percent and 39.25 percent, indicating that between 14,367,000 and 19,753,000 Africans were actually kidnapped (in round figures, of course). If such dry business does not interest the ladies (who may be preoccupied with the concerns of the Women's Movement), he can always point out that as early as 1538 the Spanish Crown directed that at least a third of the Africans taken be female—tokenism, to be sure, but at least it had an effect; by 1773 the brigantine Ann, *a slaver out of New England, was selling women for sixty-two pounds and men for only two pounds more, surely a victory for sexual equality.*

Then, having grabbed their attention, he can trot out a few specific incidents. He can tell them about the Zong *incident of 1781, in which English traders were accused of having dumped one hundred and twenty-three blacks overboard into shark-infested waters in order to claim the insurance (the charge, of course, was conspiracy to defraud). Or he can discuss the 1659 voyage of the Dutch slaver* St. Jan, *whose captain was so untalented as to have lost one hundred and ten slaves (fifty-nine men, forty-seven women, four children) to various causes (including suicide) during the Middle Passage and then, having reached the Indies, to pile his ship onto a reef and have to abandon her with the rest of his cargo (eighty-seven blacks) shackled belowdecks. By that time everybody should need another drink (except the historian, of course; historians are used to such atrocities). The party may have become a bit morose, but never fear—the historian can simply tell the amusing tale of how captains in the employ of the famed patron of exploration Prince Henry the Navigator got so busy slaving they did very little exploring, and the prince was forced to order them to refrain from actually kidnapping slaves, suggesting that they get them from native middlemen instead.*

Thus, in 1455, Prince Henry, always a visionary, became the first government official to issue regulations setting aside work for the sole profit of minority small business. That should get a laugh. [2]

Bradley's smoldering anger directed at the atrocities inflicted towards his own people, while certainly justifiable, is also directed towards dated events. You would have thought that slavery for all intents and purposes ended with the U.S. War between the States. The Civil War is generally credited as the event that abolished slavery, but that's only for those who don't take into account one Adolf Hitler.

Hitler rose to power in the 1930s promising the German people that he would deliver all that they had coming to them. So he wrote in his doctrine *Mein Kampf*, and so it was. *Mein Kampf* was a dark and doleful piece of literature spawned from a prison cell. In it Hitler blamed communism, capitalism, liberalism, and Jews for the bulk of Germany's economic and consequential social problems. From such rhetoric the Nazi party was born. Hitler ruled from 1933 to 1945, a twelve-year reign of terror within which he devastated Western Europe by war and 6 million Jews by fanatical hatred. All manner of extermination methods were employed, the most widely known being the use of gas chambers in any number of concentration camps. On September 29 and 30, 1941, however, 33,771 Jews were summarily executed in Kiev by way of machine gunning. Two things stand out. First—what kind of a world was it that would sit by and watch this monster rise to power? Over 2 million Jews were dead prior to the official start of World War II on September 3, 1939. The United States entered the war in December 1941 more out of allegiance to

Great Britain than disgust for blatant genocide. And second—it wasn't a humanistically inspired worldwide public outrage that led to his demise. It was a tactical blunder. Hitler could hardly contain himself after the ease with which he sliced through Western Europe and greedily attacked Russia in June of 1941. Trying to fight a war on two fronts is what finally did him in. His troops and resources were depleted twice as fast, and he had no friends to turn to. In a fabulous twist of poetic justice, the hunter became the hunted and (seeing the writing on the wall) he committed suicide in Berlin.

There have been other murdering savages since Hitler. Lest you doubt, let me offer up two words: Idi Amin.

Then there are those that, if they don't necessarily do the outright killing themselves, position themselves so that death surrounds them. Saddam Hussein moves about three or four times nightly, inviting himself as a "guest" into the homes of his people. These human shields provide some level of protection against the great Satan who, despite all its evilness, just can't seem to directly target innocent civilians in an attempt to blow this ruler for life to smithereens. Someone will, though, perhaps a Mideast neighbor—it's inevitable. Sadly, innocent civilians will go with him. But enough of what's happening on foreign soil. Here in America, drive-by shootings in gang-infested inner-city neighborhoods have become the order of the day. It livens up an otherwise mundane evening newscast as the rest of the country laments what's going on in LA. Only it isn't going on just in LA. Gang-related killings in 1998 in LA totaled 118, and in the rest of the American cities they totaled over 1,500. It's a national problem, this decimation of inner-city youth, and the biggest problem of all lies in the fact that it's spreading to the suburbs.

In a nation preoccupied with its internal human body

count it's hardly worth mentioning the animal body count unless, of course, you care about animals.

First, there's the generally accepted taking of interspecies life during that time of year known as "hunting season." I grew up in the rolling hills of western New York. This area has ample meadows, agricultural fields, and second-growth woodlands. All prime foraging areas and habitat for the white-tailed deer. Late every October the country roads would be lined with cars, most of which belonged to "sportsmen" from Buffalo, that metropolis of frontiersmen to the north.

These men, many of whom lacked the foresight to even discharge their guns in practice before the big hunt, were a blessing in disguise to the deer in that they usually surprised a few unfortunate members of the herd but, more often than not, drove the rest headlong into the surrounding hills. This was where the locals waited and took the larger portion of the kill. It wouldn't have been so bad, because they were, after all, locals—friends and neighbors. In my house any deer shot was skinned and quartered that day and completely butchered for consumption the next. There were few houses like our house in my town, however.

Our woodswise neighbors paraded around town with majestic bucks stretched across the hoods of their cars and trucks. Even pickups with empty beds displayed the villain deer prominently across the front hood, for why hide that which is better garishly displayed? From tavern to tavern they went, bellowing stories of hunting prowess and tracking skills while, in actuality, they discharged so many shots that they scared the poor deer to death. They stumbled home drunk but not so drunk as to forget to hang the deer openly in the maple tree out front.

By the time they sobered up and remembered that the

meat might possibly be edible, it wasn't. Enough hair had touched it to thoroughly sour the taste, so onto the outlying fields the carcasses were dumped. Great hunters these sportsmen were, and there wouldn't be much for them to do until early summer when the woodchucks would appear in the fields. Then the townies would blast away at them with scope-mounted, high-powered rifles leaned once again across the all-important hood of the family car. How much wood could a woodchuck chuck if a woodchuck had the lead of a 30-0-6 between its teeth? Nary any, I would say as I walked past twenty-three lined up and draped limp across a barbed wire fence as a once living but now dead monument to suspect riflemanship. We would shoot one every once in a while. This was in our own fields and only if their burrows did indeed endanger the legs of cattle. In addition, they made excellent meat for our hounds.

Hunting season on private (often posted) land being the self-indulgent bloodfest that it is would lead one to believe that the tormented animals might possibly fare better on public lands if for no other reason than it is public land and, as such, is subject to public outcry. Unfortunately nothing could be farther from the truth, because the public apparently feels no ownership of land that belongs (supposedly) to us all. The concept of joint or shared ownership never really caught on in America, a country where the general citizenry apparently feels that, "If I can't have it all then I don't want to share it with anyone else."

And so we all leave the stewardship of our nation's treasures to those trained to be stewards and assume that their calling also comes with a deep-seated love of nature and all things natural. Initially, this might be true, but it quickly becomes tainted with the need to make a profit, at least enough money to keep providing jobs. Public lands are leased to private interests for the purposes of raising domesticated cattle and sheep. The problem is that the other animals, the ones the public land was set aside for in the first place, are still wild and as such will take advantage of a free meal whenever it presents itself. Again, Alice Outwater from *Water*:

> *To keep the public lands safe for domesticated animals, the U.S. Department of Agriculture's Animal Damage Control Program destroys about 80,000 coyotes, 200 mountain lions, nearly 10,000 black bears, and 125,000 prairie dogs annually.* [1]

Two hundred mountain lions! I thought they were nearing endangered species classification. Ten thousand black bears? Ten thousand! They remind me of distinguished old gentlemen sitting down at the nursing home for Thanksgiving dinner. This is staggering. It's also true. One would think that animals raised for private profit should remain on private lands and that wild animals—the ones that everyone is excited to see—should remain on public land for the enjoyment of the public at large.

I am not the bleeding heart you think I am. I care more for the humans than the animals. I don't believe that the snail darter, the desert tortoise, or the bighorn sheep should adversely impact jobs, planned growth, or the infrastructure of the country. When push comes to shove, the humans come first. Species have been disappearing from the planet ever since it was a planet. While I don't want to hasten the demise of any given species, I would opt for such in a New York minute if I thought that keeping them around would in turn hasten the demise of mine.

Let me set the record straight. The snail darter, the desert tortoise, and the Santa Rosa strain of the bighorn sheep are not worth more than the livelihood of my own kind. This doesn't put me to the right of the environmental movement—it casts me out altogether. So be it.

I don't like the killing, but I will accept it if it serves a higher purpose. What I don't accept and wholeheartedly detest is the *senseless killing*. Count me out.

I'm not so much down on the true hunters and fisherman as I am the would-be hunters and fishermen that don't have a clue as to the innerworkings of natural processes or what it means to regulate game populations. Nationwide, licenses account for $400-plus million to support the U.S. Fish and Wildlife Service, conversation agencies, and state and county game wardens. Four hundred million dollars sounds like a lot of money, and you would think that more than enough would be left over for habitat restoration and/or enhancement. In truth, the bulk of the money is spent trying to capture and bring to justice poachers, those despicable individuals who ignore the laws of the land and take animals to fuel an ever-expanding black market trade.

Writes Michael Tobias in *Nature's Keepers: On the Front Lines of the Fight to Save Wildlife in America:*

> *Already the U.S. Fish and Wildlife service has set a conservative estimate of $200 million for the paid market value of illegally caught domestic animal by-products, and at least an additional $1 billion paid out by Americans to smugglers of wildlife from abroad.*
>
> *Worldwide, figures for illegally caught wildlife are estimated at between $10 and $30 billion, and the United States is the worst offender.* [3]

This is sobering news, I'll assure you, and the most embarrassing part is that I (until the advent of this book) never had an inkling that the situation was so far out of control. Tobias continues:

> *In one year, at over 25 cities in the United States (ports for smugglers), U.S. Fish and Wildlife agents confiscated over 1,000 bear carcasses and body parts of 11 different species, most of them endangered; rare mules, wood peckers, orangutans, Mongolian Bactrian camels, Indochinese hogs, 5 species of endangered sheep, and over 1,200 rare deer from Mexico to north China were recovered. But the numbers do not even intimate the wider carnage occurring. At least 95 percent of all those engaged in illegal kills get away, time after time. And for those few hunting guides and their clients, single-minded poachers, illegal occasional hunters, and weekend opportunists who do get caught, fines and/or sentencing are often so trivial as to have little ascertainable impact on the trends.* [3]

Worldwide, the poaching problem is epidemic, but why can't we Americans get the situation under control within our own borders? There are 7,000 officers across the land, with 235 of them being special agents. Their task is monumental in that there are over 7.5 million square miles of wildlife range that are under siege. That's 1,070 square miles, or 684,800 acres of land per enforcement agent. Concludes Tobias:

> *Outmaneuvered, outgunned, and vastly outnumbered, a few thousand women and men across America are fighting a war to save wildlife. Some are with the government, some in university teaching, others running nonprofit foundations or for-profit organizations, and still others are simply out there, on their own, independently trying to make a difference the best way they know how.* [3]

Unfortunately, despite everyone's best efforts to stave off extinction of some of the lower species, sometimes we fail.

The passenger pigeon is gone. It cannot be restored. This (restoration) seems to be a buzzword of the environmental movement. Wake up and smell the toast. What's gone, although regrettably, is gone. We should concentrate our efforts on keeping that which is sensible and useful among that which is left. Placing no value on the life of a species (including our own) is what got us into this environmental mess in the first place. As a nation, America has become desensitized to death. What would you expect from a country whose cinematic action heroes have nuked at least two dozen nonaction heroes before the first scene expires? We accept killing as commonplace and have taken to glorifying it. There's nothing glorious about it, though. Nothing noble. Nothing sane.

If we are to reestablish ourselves as a great people occupying a far greater country there must come a realization that God created a beauty in all creatures great and small. We must reawaken our conscience to the inherent value of life, and as an affirmation to its importance, we must strive to keep on living while we allow the other species to do the same.

Chapter Six

Ecohysteria Meets Enviroparanoia

A confused mind always says no. So does one that's misguided or misinformed. Misinformation is a close cousin to laziness. I'm as guilty of it as anyone. This is especially true in the area of politics and politicians: "Look, honey. There's another pompous ass spewing forth some meaningless speech on the TV. Oh God! There must be some ball game somewhere on this thing. Even the all-English lawn bowling championships would be better than this. Oh for crying out loud. There's another one of those crackpot environmentalists going on about God only knows what!"

The Green Decade has picked up a lot of freeloaders and leeches. They're well intentioned—some of them. They're camera hogs and glorymongers—a lot of them. In a genre given high visibility it is easy for one to become visible and gobble up all the credit. For this reason (a readily accessible limelight), not too surprisingly, entertainers and movie stars have apparently taken it upon themselves to save the planet.

Cheryl Tiegs (I had her bikinied poster on my wall when

I was single) wants to save the elephants in east Africa. Other actors are concerned about the fate of the snow leopards. If any one of them could give me genus and species and a few vital statistics about life history and morphology I would be mildly impressed. But I would bet you even money that they can't. Oh, they could queue up for the camera and tell you about the terrible, awful things that are happening to these wonderful creatures. They would ask for your support and donations, the latter being considerably more important. None of them, I am quite sure, could or would give you a pitch to save a subspecies of Homo sapiens, especially the American strain, that beleaguered clan known as real estate developers.

In my business, landscape architecture, commissions, which constitute survival, ultimately depend on the growth of the built environment. Without those strip shopping centers and housing tracts Johnny is a very dull (and extremely poor) boy. True, sweeping change is called for in the design arena to make these elements more attractive, and we will address that issue in the next chapter. Truer still, without these elements there is little designing to do, and I have to contemplate a career shift. I sit at my drafting board armed with dictionary and thesaurus rather than pen and pencil. I don't like it one bit.

The American Society of Landscape Architects recommends pursuing environmental commissions such as cleaning up landfills and turning former strip mine areas into public parks. Noble commissions, I assure you, but few and far between. The definition of landscape architecture, generated by God only knows who, originates with some gobbledygook until it arrives at what is generally considered to be the thrust of the profession: "Stewardship of the land . . . for its highest and best purpose." Putting aside just what this purpose might be for the moment, let's examine the issue of land. We don't own it. We can't impact the use of the Earth to a higher ideal if we can't get into the game. Unless you intend on being an unsolicited or uncommissioned environmental activist or political lobbyist (a sure path to starvation), a sponsor is needed.

It's like joining a country club; there's only one way in—by invitation only. The only way I do design work and thus influence environmental quality and the seen landscape is if a landowner hires me. Therefore, I try not to look upon them as greedy land barons or despoilers of the environment, although occasionally, I must admit, they are both. I look upon them as holders of a small piece of the bigger Earth that I care so much about. As such, they are individuals to be led and swayed gently down the path of environmental righteousness.

The no-growthers in the cities and the preservationists beyond their fringes have a "do nothing and nothing bad is likely to happen" mentality. There is population growth in America. While not an explosion, as in the rest of the world, our numbers increase. Growth is inevitable. Like Ian McHarg, who wrote the classic man-cooperating-with-nature manual *Design with Nature,* I subscribe to the theory of planned growth in land areas that will best accommodate it.

Deal with reality on environmental terms rather than say that reality must step aside for the good of the environment. Rather than burying their heads in the sand, which would be the proper manifestation of their beliefs, they procure positions on planning commissions, city councils, and state review agencies. So entrenched, the economic power of their no-growth mentality can have far-reaching and catastrophic effects. They cite concern for the environment when turning down development proposal upon development proposal. To hear them talk you would think they have a deep-seated knowledge of biology and ecology. The real biologists and ecologists, those individuals with enough training and credentials to inspire the developer to bring them in to support his position, just have to laugh at them.

First, the self-appointed eco-elite try to discredit the real estate developer and building professionals in general as one-dimensional simpletons so motivated by a quick buck that they couldn't possibly understand the myriad of complex innerworkings and interrelationships of the environment.

Oh really? Filing environmental impact reports. Riding herd on a plethora of squabbling designers to carve out a set of incoherent, incongruent working drawings. Pulling permits. Lining up subcontractors. Dealing with belligerent, crazed building inspectors. Lien releases. Bank vouchers. Bank charges. Bounced checks. Labor relations. Unemployment disputes. Workman's compensation. Owners who slither and squirm out of paying up at the end of the job. Trying to access profits (if there are any). The Internal Revenue Service. Supplier increases without notification. And, the last time he looked on his trucks, it was readily apparent that his employees were robbing him blind. Is this the greedy opportunist they're talking about?

Environmental intellectuals, one and all, *get off his back*. The man understands complex interrelationships, quite possibly far better than you or I. Whoever said that business was easy was definitely not a businessman. The builder understands the concepts of the food web, nutrient cycles, habitat, and species diversification; it's just that he doesn't understand you. In his eyes he's building something the public desperately wants, while you're building a mountain out of a molehill.

Second, the eco-aristocracy tries to take him on. Throw

another log on the fire as far as he's concerned. He's used to not overreacting to any one threat. He takes harassment in stride. An emergency is 911. Everything else will have to wait until he gets to it.

Third, the eco-nobility tries to stop him. Now they've crossed the line into a no-holds-barred barroom brawl. While they piss and moan about how endangered species can't survive his insensitive destructive ways, he grits his teeth and shakes his head in amazement, for they have made a cardinal mistake. Don't they know that they're talking about survival to a *survivor*?

The real estate developer, despite the mounting opposition, has an instinct to build programmed deep inside him. Like geese flying south for the winter, salmon swimming upstream to spawn, bears hibernating, wildflower seeds sprouting in spring, and the leaves of deciduous trees dropping in the fall, the builder must build—it's in his nature. Like a mountain lion protecting her cubs, he has an almost maternal instinct towards the construction process. It's who he is, and if you think that you're going to stop him you had better be ready to put up your dukes.

When push comes to shove most people and entities won't cross that tenacious line, so they settle for trying to slow him down. For the most part, they've become quite adept at it.

In California, that mecca for bitching and whining, no large-scale development project will be considered without first being scrutinized for environmental compatibility. The vehicle used to make, or more frequently break, the developer's case is called an Environmental Impact Statement (EIS) on the national level and an Environmental Impact Report (EIR) on the state level. For simplicity's sake, let's just call it an Environmental Report. The format is usually, more or less, the same. There's an introduction, proposed project description, environmental analysis, alternatives to development, and some sort of a conclusion. They range widely in substance and content, depending most heavily on the size of the fee garnered by the preparing agency. They usually take a year to eighteen months to assemble and frequently just as long to review. This puts the real estate developer in the position of having to start three years early to reach the day when he can put his first shovel in the ground. This is if he's approved, with the odds currently running at six to one against him. What's worse, from his point of view, is that he's expected to fish into his own pocket to pay all of those who wrote the fatalistic report in the first place. It's a little like buying ammunition for the person who's holding the gun that's pointed at your head.

One would naturally assume that wherever this money goes, coercion and boodle would soon follow. For this reason (an implied vested interest), reports with favorable findings towards the proposed development are looked at with contempt by the environmentally concerned public at large. When a report issues a negative finding, it's generally thought that the worst elements have been glossed over and the development must be *really bad*. But the truth of the matter is that when you study any number of reports in any given development genre they all look and read remarkably alike. When further defined to specific geographic regions this identity crisis becomes even more acute. Accounting for the bulk of the sameness is that the same compiling firms are usually selected.

They bring in the same consultants who regurgitate on-hand, boilerplate information. Mitigation measures are most often long on suggestions for infusions of soothing healing cash and short on any original form of thought.

By the necessity to appear authoritative, Environmental

Reports are always inordinately thick. If they don't rival the size of the family bible they're looked at with disdain. Remember, however, that this tome did not take centuries to write; it took months, or for any given consulting entity—weeks. This is not the stuff of great literature, not even the makings of good journalism. The ultimate goal is to generate enough verbiage to fill enough pages to thoroughly intimidate reviewers into skimming rather than reading. In short—garbage in, garbage out.

It's all garbage as far as the developer is concerned, and sometimes he has a point. Besides the environmental analysis paralysis, how realistic are the alternatives to development? First is the no-development strategy, which is wholeheartedly embraced by the no-growth community until they are hit with the big but. The big but plays into the lesser of two evils mentality, with the ploy being that if we don't develop it someone else will, and they won't do as good a job. Says who? Says them. Incredibly, a lot of times it works.

Then there's my personal favorite—the three alternative site studies. This is where pie-in-the-sky and pulp fiction merge to produce site plans of huge, unrealistic densities on land that isn't even owned. As if the developer is really going to consider doing this. The alternative site studies are futile in nature and a complete waste of time in actuality because they have no basis in reality. One gander at the alternative proposals and the current proposal starts to look like a land use messiah.

Do EIRs help? Well, they certainly make for a longer period of time to get a project approved. With the time increase, one would think that there could be more time dedicated to initial creative design. There could be, only there isn't. The developer isn't going to commit any outlay of monies until he has a viable project, and the design firm isn't going to pour its creative juices into a project that could literally die on the vine. No, the Environmental Report process is a master of time suckage quite unlike any other paper chase. The way the real estate developer looks at it, it doesn't matter if the government wants an EIR, an EIS, or an EIEIO. In the end, money will conquer all. It's just a matter of time.

The way I look at it, it seems like a lot of money that could be used (or donated) to serve higher environmental purposes is just plain wasted in paying paper homage to the governmental machine. The process precludes the small to midsize developer who doesn't have the financial backing to stay in the hunt. What we're left with is big construction business butting heads with big government, and the only ones making any real money are the attorneys representing both.

Nowhere on the four corners of the Earth does a development proposal stir up as much scuttlebutt and outrage as does environmental public enemy number one—the private eighteen-hole championship golf course. The closer the course gets to a hillside, the more the fur flies.

The first negative impact, the opposition asserts, comes in the area of habitat destruction. This is true for the short term, but what many detractors fail to realize is that courses also *provide habitat.* Often times they contribute more acreage of usable habitat than they originally disturbed. This is particularly true in the Southwest, where the introduction of water will always create a flourish of flora and fauna. In the final analysis, animal populations in particular will increase at the fringe areas of the course. Plant species and the life spans of annuals will increase. In short, a golf course is rarely an environmental despoiler, while it's frequently an environmental enhancer. This is especially true in the area of water conservation. Turf loves sand, and golf courses are built with a lot of it. This turf and underlying sand, respectively, act as soil surface and substrate filters, which aid in purifying water as it percolates through the soil. This filtering action works so well that gray water and brown water can be utilized to irrigate courses. Finding uses for not so potable yet readily available secondary water resources is a godsend in the West. With impure water skipping one or two steps in the purifying process, the existing wastewater sanitary facilities are less taxed and better able to more quickly and efficiently treat the water they do receive.

Golf courses offer up an ecological win-win situation, which is a good thing because the popularity of the game is increasing fivefold every decade, while conversely, the number of courses will only increase by about 10 percent over the same time frame. Forget about soccer; golf is the new international game. Besides, a biweekly visit to the links is as close to the wild as a lot of people will ever get. While they are an oversimplification of biodiversity, golf courses are still living, viable, natural systems. They sure beat asphalt and concrete.

Housing. The need for shelter. Land ownership with all the trappings of history and the responsibility it entails. While increasingly less achievable, to own one's own home is still the American dream. How to settle upon the land yet still allow its life systems to continue is one of the great design challenges of our times. In some areas, the deserts and chaparrals in particular, we appear to be finally up to the task.

It all started outside Phoenix, Arizona. A forward-thinking land developer named Lyle Anderson enlisted the services of a visionary land planner named Gage Davis. A prototype to what an environmentally sound housing tract should be was born at Desert Highlands. In a triumvirate of private enterprise (the developer), a governmental entity (the city of

Scottsdale, Arizona), and the environment (low elevation Sonora Desert), a building scenario which recognized the uniqueness of all three was devised.

The individual home lots were to be left undisturbed at their periphery, with only the driveway apron penetrating through the protective outer ring. An area inside the outer ring and closing onto itself is classified as the "building envelope." This is where the action is. In a landmark compilation of meaningful legislation, the city of Scottsdale holds these envelopes collectively as public easements. As such, they will not release an easement to an eventual land purchaser until he/she has done what the city dictates, which is to identify and inventory all significant trees and cacti. The land purchaser is then required to dig up and stockpile this vegetation in a holding yard until such time as a structure is built and the plant material is returned, if not to its original home, at least to its original site. In the early eighties this was the cutting edge in environmentally sensitive site development. Over time it gave rise to the theory of *site-specific* collections of vegetative and nonvegetative (rocks, boulders) site elements. This helped to ensure that the resultant development eventually would look like it grew out of the existing environment rather than having rolled through it. While initially looked upon as a massive undertaking of counterproductive mitigation procedures, the results proved a smashing success.

First, mycorrhizal fungi which lived in the transplanted root-balls reestablished themselves more quickly. Second, small-scale niches were preserved, which when combined, allowed for full-scale habitat restoration. Third, it was discovered that with rapidly improving devegetation methodologies, the cost of replanting a mature landscape competed quite favorably with the cost of installing a new landscape.

The detractors to the program immediately pointed out that the life spans of the older transplanted trees would not match the life span of spanking new nursery-grown trees. They had a point but missed the much larger or more important point. Naturally recurring succession is an environmental process that influences population dynamics of the organisms in the ecosystem. By interrupting the time frame of a cycle, organisms whose peak production periods occur within that span would be adversely affected. This seems like a minor point, but in nature, it's huge. In other words, the ecosystem would be less diverse because it would be starting from scratch. A lack of biodiversity in any given ecosystem opens up the entire whole to outside attacks of pestilence and disease.

This is what all those boring textbooks mean when they talk about the *balance of nature*.

It's the fundamental law of human nature that that which we are forced to do often has a more far-reaching impact than that which we should do if for no other reason than we actually do it. The Desert Highlands project was groundbreaking, as was the way the city of Scottsdale helped to turn biological theory into law. It served as a model for similar projects throughout the West. One of the most interesting aspects in all of this is that the residents of these environmentally mandated communities, many of whom felt initially inconvenienced to the point of accusing infringement of their personal rights, became by necessity much more environmentally aware and ultimately turned into the staunchest supporters of future similar programs.

Can man live within nature? Of course he can, if the choice is to live this way or not live at all. It all boils down to a restructuring of attitudes. Sure, we as a species, because of our God-given intelligence, can dominate the Earth. We have shown our propensity to do this time and time again. Patterns of land ownership which equate to Earth ownership must change. We need more on-site trees. We need fewer walls, which would allow for an increase in wildlife corridors. As trite as it seems to say—we need to live and let live.

Ecohysteria is rooted in the belief that man must be kept away from nature in order to protect it from his destructive ways. Enviroparanoia stems from the historical fact that we have hacked, shot, paved, dredged, polluted, and wasted every gift of nature that we've been presented with and probably will again. Like the saying goes, "Just because you're paranoid doesn't mean they're not out to get you." Pulling these two groups of far-left environmentalists back to the middle will be just as difficult as reawakening the environmentally apathetic mainstream who occupy the right.

A confused mind always says no, so let's end the confusion. There is only one Earth on which to live environmentally right, wrong, or indifferent. In the seventies people would somewhat self-righteously say, "If you're not part of the solution, you're part of the problem." It may have struck a chord, but it played a sour note. Today, if you're not part of the solution, you're part of the inevitable extinction. It, likewise, strikes a chord, but the vast majority of us seem to be confused about which note to play next.

No wonder the hysterical, paranoid, environmental left is so worked up.

And then there is the population at large, the environmental right, who don't even know there is an environmental movement. The men and women in the street, if you will. These people talk about "the environment" as if it was a county park miles or even farther away from their home—something they would like to visit and quite possibly enjoy sometime in the near future. A place where they would like to take the kids if they ever get a day off. Until they come to the realization that they are sitting smack-dab in the middle of the environment they will never get it. Until it dawns on them that the toilet bowl connects to the hydrological cycle, that hairspray goes into the atmosphere, that cigarette butts are not readily biodegradable, they will remain clueless. The clueless majority, because they're neutral, can't help. This leaves us with those who do have an opinion, cause, or vested interest. This is the crux of the problem with the environmental issue in the United States. People either lean too far to the left or too far to the right. They are either so deep in the forest that they can't see the trees or they won't go near the forest at all.

Chapter Seven

What the Public Sees

Cigarette smoking is a filthy, disgusting habit. Aside from the obvious health risks—lung cancer and air pollution—there's the visual pollution. There's a girl that works at the office next to mine that's forced by her coworkers to take her cigarette break outside. She apparently feels that the planter across from their front doorway is her personal ashtray and has taken to contributing about eight butts a day to a rapidly expanding pile. I suppose that she'll eventually work her way around the building, because far be it for her to actually notice that it's a visual inconvenience. I've taken a solemn vow not to pick up after her. It's stubbornness, really, because I pick up candy wrappers, soda cups, pop bottles, beer and wine bottles, and, yes, even cigarette wrappers and packs. It's just the butts that get to me. Like I'll be the butt end of a much larger joke if I actually do this. And so the pile grows as sort of a heaped sculptural tribute to the fact that litter is acceptable to those who don't want to be too personally inconvenienced.

Unfortunately, that would be the greater majority of the population.

Where did all the antilitter campaigns of the seventies go? Did we just give up? There's more paper and trash lying around than ever before. Save for our beaches and highways, there doesn't seem to be any concentrated clean-up effort. It'd be nice to see an "Adopt a Street Corner" or "Clean a City Block" program. They are long overdue.

Recycling was all the rage in the early eighties. Some cities even issued color-coded waste receptacles. Green for plastic, blue for glass, yellow for paper. Most of the citizenry found all the sorting and categorizing to be a royal pain in the ass. There was a run on black plastic trash bags. One color excepted all. The problem was out of sight and out of mind until it hit the landfill. The problem reverts to an office function as simple as who will do the billing? For without cash flow, an office dies. And without trash pick-up, a county becomes buried in its own wastes.

What the public sees, to a large extent, affects who they are or are about to become. Litter is an obvious offender, but there are other less noticeable yet more significant contributors to the visual pollution that engulfs our nation. Junk, decaying mobile homes, and gaudy signage along the roadsides and highways. Gaudier signage still in the cities, all vying for our attention yet confusing us to the point where we tune them out for the sake of clarity. But providing the mind with visual clarity deprives the senses. They atrophy and die. We walk through life with blinders on. Like the wings of birds not utilized for flying, will our eyes evolve to mere appendages that have not yet fallen off? Will they become one-way receptors of television sets and computer screens? Will the only thing we notice with our gift of vision be sporting events, girlie magazines, and piles of unpaid bills?

Will we not notice the grandeur of land and water, the greatness of heroic architecture, the intimacy of a small urban park? Will our vision become as dysfunctional as the emotional growth of children in an alcoholic home? Yes. It's already happening. The visual pollution and the substandard graphic presentation of the nation's signmakers are living up to our low expectations.

Our internal survival mechanism always rules out over our unexpressed quality of life aspirations. Better to create an orderly world within the four interior walls of our homes and apartments than to demand a higher external cleanliness standard.

We don't like what we see when we leave our homes so much that we've decided to stay in. With the advent of the Home Shopping Network, video rentals, telebanking, et cetera, we, as a society, are leaving our homes less. A new fad has developed, and like all fads, it's been given a title. "Home Cocooning" is the new buzzword used to describe a home-locked society. As with all terms used to deny growing problems, it puts the best light on the fading sociability of a nation. It should be called what it is—acute national agoraphobia. And it's getting worse.

The movie industry has responded with the Cineplex, while shopping centers have become malls, which become power centers, which become shopping carnivals. It takes a big hook to snatch us from our easy chairs. Or it takes Mondays.

The commuter society will be in their cars, subways, or buses come the start of the work week. They will choose the shortest distance between two points to get to work. This is to save on gas or travel expense but most frequently because they are running late. The route most often takes them into the city centers or to the outlying light industrial parks. Along the way they will be visually deluged with billboards, advertisements, and window displays.

They'll tune all this out, of course, until they reach the workplace. Then they'll really shut down. The Worko sapiens won't be human again until later that evening, when they once again hit their easy chairs. The American public at large is allowing itself to be herded like sheep into a lifestyle where it thinks it's in control but where people are really prisoners under self-inflicted house arrest. The only difference is that the term of incarceration has no limit.

Instead of demanding more from the built environment, we readily accept less. Our city centers are not the great cultural magnets that they could be but rather ghost towns after five o'clock. The signs that line the streets are not short-lived works of art but rather large-scale screaming trash on the vertical plane that make it so easy to accept the smaller-scale underlying trash on the ground plane.

How can we as a people even begin to talk about the vast environmental problems lying underneath and over the Earth's surface when we can't even keep that which we can readily see and touch clean?

Part of the problem is that we are such a consumptive society. Is it any wonder, given what we go through, that there is so much litter and urban blight? And it doesn't stop at the city line. Out in the country the trash may be more spread out, but where it does occur, it's larger in scale. Indeed, America is a nation being buried in its own wastes, and the only solution (besides a better clean-up effort) is to create less stuff.

Recycling, for all its good intentions, has a lot of logistic problems, not the least of which is that it's cost prohibitive. A better solution is not to create so much garbage in the first place. In 1998 Robert Lilienfeld and William Rathje published *Use Less Stuff: Environmental Solutions for Who We Really Are.* It's a great little manual based on the simple premise to reduce consumption and reuse that which has been consumed. It is a different theory than recycling because *nothing changes*. It's either not bought or not so readily thrown away. The theory has been around a long time in other forms. Athletes are taught to push away from the training table while they still feel a little hungry. Their body metabolism can't quite process the food energy immediately. Once they stop eating, in short order, their bodies catch up to their hunger and the available energy is better utilized. We waste a lot of food, especially during those massive holiday dinners. If we cooked and prepared less, more of what is on the table would get eaten. There would be less plastic wrapper required for the leftovers which are usually thrown out in the course of a week anyway.

Refillable containers as opposed to disposable ones are the order of the day. Note that refilling is different than recycling in that the container stays in the possession of the consumer and remains in its original form. This is different than recycled plastics and aluminum, where energy must be utilized when they are melted down and reconfigured.

This is the thrust of the *Use Less Stuff* program—to recognize real needs and develop strategies that limit waste at the point of consumption rather than deal with the effects of needless overconsumption. Rarely do we ever need as much as we think we do. How many times have we triple-overpacked for a weekend trip? This illustrates the difference between real and imagined need. Americans are like giant packrats, acquiring hair blowers, baby strollers, and lawn mowers. Any given middle-class household has more than its fair share of items that it either didn't need, grew out of needing, wore out, broke down, or forgot about. Our drive to acquire that which we don't need is a hybrid form of kleptomania whereby we have no overt intention to harm the environment yet it loses anyways because something is taken. Raw materials and energy are used to create stuff, and the only way to slow the process is to demand less of the end products.

Here are just a few suggestions and some practical advice from the conclusion of *Use Less Stuff:*

> Driving your car. *If everyone drove one day less per month and saved two gallons of gasoline each time, we'd reduce total annual gasoline consumption by 1.5 billion gallons and carbon dioxide production by 16.5 million tons. (We would also save about $30.00 each.)*
>
> Food Waste. *If every single one of us wasted one less ounce of food per week, it would reduce annual food waste by 750 million pounds.*
>
> Packaging Waste. *Using one less sheet of paper per day at your office cuts your personal consumption by half a ream, or 250 sheets, per year. That's about 5 pounds you've saved. In a typical company with 1,000 employees, that equals 2.5 tons of paper that isn't used—saving trees, water, and energy while reducing pollution and greenhouse gas emissions.*
>
> *We're not saying that you should do everything we suggest. But please do something. For starters, pick things that save you the most money. Just remember that every time you save financial resources, we all save natural resources. That's a win-win situation that's as easy on the planet as it is on your wallet.*
>
> *It is also a win-win situation for our civilization. If everyone would decide to follow just a few suggestions, then the results would be visible—IMMEDIATELY.*

This is a new kind of environmentalism, what we call environmentalism for who we really are. *If we listen to it and take it seriously, it is the best way for us to become the first culture in the history of the world to learn to use less stuff—in time to continue to survive where others have collapsed.* [4]

America is a beautiful country, as is evidenced by her national parks—Grand Canyon, Great Smoky Mountains, Grand Teton, Yellowstone, and Yosemite to name but a few. The national monuments—Montezuma Castle, Canyon de Chelly, Sequoia, and Joshua Tree, among others, rival the loveliness if not the size of the parks. The catch is that 95 percent of the population lives far away from such magnificence. Three-quarters of the country will never see even *one* of the aforementioned paradises. They're left to deal with that which is at their immediate disposal. Not everyone can recreate the power of the Grand Teton mountain range in their backyard. Even with loads of cash, Disney's Matterhorn pales in comparison to the real thing. The built and subsequently landscaped environment is an interpretation or much smaller-scale emulation of the grandeur of nature. If we can't copy, perhaps we can distract. We embellish with architectural motifs, storefront facades, fountains, street lamps, and that great cure-all—public art. Does art transcend nature? Hardly. The great majority of it does not complement and rarely does it compete with natural beauty.

So what creates beauty in our lives once we close our front doors behind us? An ordering and simplification of the environment. Up close, nature does not always stay beautiful. Fields of spring wildflowers wafting in the breeze will turn to decaying low-lying brush by midsummer. A deep, forested area would allow very little light or wind circulation on a suburban lot. Many mountain streams run dry after all the snow has melted in spring. Nature is often perceived as being far more beautiful than she really is, if only for the fact that, like a supermodel, she is only photographed at the height of her makeup. While the built landscape cannot achieve such fantastic highs, it is not allowed such lows. It is expected to perform at an average level of acceptance year-round. Nature doesn't concern herself with year-round beauty, but the built landscape must. That which lies and otherwise resides outside the realm of truly natural must have enough interest to capture our attention and remind us of all things natural, wild, and free. This realization is comforting to us and, in a subliminal way, reminds us that nature and the environment are always with us, although we will not always be with it. It's the time element that's so critical. We most deeply appreciate that which we are in immediate jeopardy of losing.

Perhaps it's an issue of newness in America. Europe is quaint because her cities have been around for thousands of years. Buildings are literally built on top of the ruins of other ones. The urban edge and countryside have aged and crumbled into one another so many times that it's hard to distinguish where one ends and the other begins. America is different. Her cities were thrown together hastily, and before the urban fabric could evolve, a freeway was cut through it. It would be nice to go back and have a do-over, but that won't happen because this isn't where the wealth is. It lies in the suburbs or in the exclusive country clubs. Five percent of the population hoards 95 percent of all the wealth. Behind the walls of those exclusive gated communities lies what the public doesn't see. The best design, the best construction, the best of everything. We can resent it as we analyze why it's so successful. There is no litter, homes are kept up, and people feel secure enough behind those walls to display prized sculptures and artifacts in their front yards. Above all else, *the place is clean*. They have hired help to pick up after them. We will have to pick up after ourselves.

America needs a national face-lift and a national clean-up effort, but what she really needs is a national awareness that the country can't clean itself, so the population must. It is a sad fact, and this is key, that what the public sees is a mirror image of what the public is.

Chapter Eight

One Man - One Life

The Earth will never be what it once was. She experiences an aging process similar to our own human aging process. While slower, measured in centuries versus years, there is essentially the same net result. Things change and cannot be reversed. The future is tenuous.

Resources are depleted. Fossil fuels will run out. Pure water becomes more scarce while the air bulges with pollutants. Alternative environmental lifestyles are the order of the day. Concentration on providing a future for the children of the world will lead to the realization that we are obligated to stabilize the Earth, and once it is stable, we must recognize the natural processes and intellectual belief systems that should be nurtured and instilled in order to hold the biomes of the Earth in a steady state.

Environmental sustainability versus man-made profitability. The survival of the masses versus the wealth of a few. Humanistically, to choose between the two seems like a no-brainer, except that we all want to be rich. Ah, greed.

Avaricious appetites for a higher station in life leads to a hostile world.

The more civilized countries, the first-world nations, if you will, camouflage their true intentions by propping up governments that pretend to be fair to all. First the politicians get rich. Then their faithful supporters. Then, the fringe elite. The manufacturers, the suppliers, the organizers of legalities and records. Professional athletes and entertainers. Then comes a middle class, born of necessity, to care for the upper three classes and excessively overcharge the others. The doctors, builders, automobile mechanics, and cable providers. The guilty know who they are. Then comes the lower middle class. The worker bees so accurately depicted in beer commercials. Those poor slobs that you just have to love because they pay everyone else's taxes. Then comes the lower class. The truly poor. The destitute.

The second world. The less civilized but somewhat more festive countries seem to get by on less. There's an upper, middle, and lower class. The poor are not talked about. The destitute disappear into the cracks of the sidewalks. As long as they can get along with the big boys, rape their land, and aspire for entry into the first world they seem to maintain a comfortable status quo. At least there's hope in such a country. Something big could actually happen. Even with graft and suspect accounting practices they have enough money in their coffers to support a military with planes and tanks and ships. This makes the first world nervous and the third world anxious to see some kind of shake-up that could possibly brighten up their miserable lives.

The third world. The cheap seats high in the nosebleed section. Too far from the playing field, economically, to really get into the game. There are no sidewalks to provide cracks for the destitute to fall into—they die in streets. Sadly, the infant mortality rate is measured in deaths per hundreds rather than thousands. There are a few rich. Emperors, dictators, drug dealers, any thug with a machine gun mounted on a jeep. Everyone else is poor.

We know who we are and who we would like to be. The basic human desire to attain a better station in life (no matter how good the current one is) is the common denominator of all mankind. All people, even those that are definitely good or evil, have a few things in common. They must eat, drink, and breathe in order to live. And they instinctively love their children because God made us that way if for no other reason than to insure survival of the species. Therefore the majority of the people across the globe struggle to survive and try to lessen what, they feel, will be their children's struggle to survive.

From such thin threads of commonality, the peoples of the Earth must attempt to weave a vibrant tapestry of international ecopolicy. This often discussed and frequently lamented forthcoming policy will be compelled to establish a goal-orientated global agenda which will define the minimum acceptable levels of various forms of pollution, human and animal birth rates, and the quantity and quality of set-aside, protected acreages of forests, grasslands, swamps, shorelines, and waterways. If only we could get all the peoples, nations, tribes, and kings to agree on this minimal point of departure—oh, what a wonderful world it would be. There's been attempts, albeit few and far between, with rather abysmal results.

Earth Day, April 22, attempts to provide an awareness of the environment. With no war in Vietnam, no sexual revolution, no generational upheaval to cling to (as with my age group), this is what the twentysomething crowd now has as a cause and a chance to define their generation. While every other generation feels its successor's pales in comparison, this new generation of emerging adults is hip if somewhat jaded. *Rolling Stone* magazine's recently (1998) televised "State of the Union" did not portray a very optimistic or positive disposition among young people. The economic outlook, in particular, appeared bleak. The point of greatest disenchantment was that this generation will not live as well as the last. What they're too young to realize is that that generation, the fortysomethings, did not live as well as their parents, the sixtysomethings. Computers take potential jobs away. Robotics, likewise, take potential jobs away. Apathy contributes to potential jobs going unrealized.

Motivation is born of action and not the other way around. Nothing positive ever happened to anyone sitting around and waiting for it to. A belief that first one will get motivated and then they will take action is nothing more than a belief; it has nothing to do with reality. Motivate means to actuate (start up), while momentum means impetus (a driving force). Thus one is cause while the other is effect. This is as key as understanding which came first—the chicken or the egg. Action must be taken, often with no idea of what results to reasonably expect, before any form of energy can be generated. The sixtysomethings are tired and are not going to lend much more to the environmental movement than donations and sage advice. The fortysomethings are beleaguered with debt and disillusionment. They gave it a hell of a go when they were younger. Earth Day, after all, was born in 1970 and inspired several noteworthy environmental advances before fizzling out by the mid-eighties into nothing more than a celebration of past accomplishments. But the environmental movement cannot rest on its hippy-dippy laurels. It needs a shot in the arm. The fortysomethings pushed the ecovehicle as hard and as fast as they could, but now it and they have run out of gas.

Which brings us to the twentysomethings—the hope for the future. Here's a great big news flash. *The future is now.* Stop giving despondent, morose interviews to *Rolling Stone* magazine and seize the biggest opportunity of your young, lackluster lives. Every generation has its authors, poets, singers, and leaders. Yes, every generation has its comeuppance, and this is yours. With the fall of Russia and the failure of any Mideastern crackpot dictator to make a credible effort to replace her as a threat, what's the biggest menace facing young Americans today? Environmental collapse on the one hand and the crumbling of the country's infrastructure on the other. And the two are intrinsically linked. Each, in some way, shape, or form can enhance the other.

There's jobs aplenty at the root of these two issues. Let's let history repeat itself and return to the days of FDR's Job Corps. Let's turn the youth that are to inherit the Earth loose on her impending repair. And, even more importantly, once repaired, let's devise a reasonable process for her maintenance and upkeep. America, as a nation, has a tendency to let things get to crisis proportions before recognizing the need to take swift and decisive action. Once we do what is necessary to back away from the rapidly approaching edge let's vow never to live so close to it again.

How do we get there from here? By laying down the law. By letting it be known that this is what we want and voting in political platforms that promise to deliver the goods. And just as quickly voting them out when and if they don't. The problem lies where it always has. It's one thing to make demands on our politicians, who invariably empathize with our desires.

But when empathy doesn't equate to meaningful action, it's four years of frustration over inaction or broken promises before we can do anything about the betrayal.

While it may be unrealistic to expect to shorten the presidential term, as it usually takes eighteen months to two years before a new regime can free itself from the shackles of the old one, it's not unrealistic to restructure other political posts—especially the now appointed Secretary of the Interior. With environmental issues becoming increasingly more pressing, this position needs more scrutiny. First, it should be changed to an elected position, and second, the term should not exceed two years. Far-ranging and broad-sweeping environmental proposals could be put on the biannual ballot. This one simple change could dramatically alter national ecopolicy and force the creation of jobs that benefit the environment.

Then there's the need to generate capital to fuel the job-creation juggernaut. Let's turn to the richest, most powerful arm of our government—the IRS. If we can dedicate one dollar of our tax refunds to political war chests, why not be able to dedicate up to five dollars for an environmental trust fund? While we're at it, I suppose the same thing could be said for education, law enforcement, etc. Anything's possible.

But, to be realists, we must look at what's probable. Remember President Reagan's trickle-down theory? How much of the supposed internal wealth, the unseen, unflaunted motherload, if you will, trickled down to you? Let's not waste our time hoping for contributions from the private sector. Greed and cynicism, being what they are, will quell this noble notion before it ever gets started. Let's devise a vehicle to make it happen.

The individual person, the man in the street, the everyday Joe, looks at the environmental problems afflicting the planet and just throws up his hands in disgust. Acid rain, global warming, the hole in the ozone layer, solid waste disposal, and, above all else, the rapidly expanding world population around him. What can he do? He's just one man with one life. First he looks for leadership from the obvious leaders in his own land. Vice President Al Gore (then Senator Al Gore) produced *Earth in the Balance.* It was copyrighted in 1992, just when the presidential campaign with the republican incumbent George Bush started to heat up. It was quickly reprinted with a new forward twelve months later in 1993. In this version, immediately from the get-go, not even out of the new forward, Gore blasts the Bush administration for virtually sabotaging the first Earth Summit held in Rio de Janeiro, Brazil in June of 1992. When Bush's people failed to act on the major issues, especially those concerning CO_2 levels in the atmosphere, virtually every other world power followed suit. Shame on you, George. Undaunted, the Summit drew up a pact of several treaties with some global impact, but when it came to the big one (CO_2 levels), the U.S. refused to sign. Gore paints a picture that the U.S. was embarrassed by its unwavering conservatism and staunch support for all things profitable if not particularly environmentally sound.

Scathing criticism indeed and probably well deserved. But there's a subplot to all of this that, because of what it illustrates, overshadows the importance of the main plot. The Clinton/Gore team did come to power in 1992, and Gore, in particular, now being the captain of his own ship, could have easily pushed for another Earth Summit, perhaps hosted on U.S. soil. So how many Earth Summits have there been since that maiden voyage in Rio? Exactly zero! Shame on you, Al. People who live in glass houses shouldn't throw stones.

Former Washington state governor Dixy Lee Ray, primarily as a heated response to Gore's forerunning papers and speeches which were to comprise *Earth in the Balance,* wrote *Trashing the Planet.* Nothing to worry about, writes Dixy. In a rehashing of an often-heard phrase from the early seventies, she assures us that science and technology got us into this mess and science and technology will get us out. I can't personally fathom logic that basically says, "Let's now trust those that have previously proven themselves untrustworthy." In other words, let's let the inmates run the asylum. Governor Ray repeatedly hammers home the point that science and technology are so complex and those that comprise these careers are so omnipotent that our fears are miniscule in comparison. She acts as if they are the adults and we are the children that should trust their every word because—well, because they just plain know more. The only thing is that we are not children, and on top of that, if the scientists and technologists are so damned smart, how come they didn't see this environmental crisis (that *does* exist) coming in the first place?

So much for the politicians, except to say that with leadership like this, God help us all. Which brings us back to the individual. We separately must adopt the attitude that if we want the job done right then we must do it ourselves. In this vein, consider that without the benefit of a sizeable publisher's advance, with no team of research assistants or ghost writers, with no name recognition to immediately thrust them onto the national best-seller list, two environmental writers have risen above the finger pointing and rhetoric to write books that actually do reflect a deep-seated understanding and love for the environment. Yes, there are some new prophets to turn to.

The aforementioned and oft-quoted Alice Outwater's *Water* is certainly a classic. In less than half the space of Gore's or Ray's books she says twice as much. Then there's David

Quammen, a voice crying from the wilderness of the Montana outback. His *Natural Acts,* a collection of articles from *Outdoor* magazine, sizzles with enlightenment, while *Song of the Dodo* is a well-written, thoroughly researched account of animal evolution and extinction as displayed on islands. Taking a cue from Charles Darwin and Alfred Russell Wallace, it is well known among naturalists that islands, because they are isolated from larger land masses, make excellent living laboratories in which to study creatures, biological interrelationships, habitats, niches, and the dynamics of extinctions. In twice the pages of the national best sellers, Quammen provides ten times the knowledge, and he did it the old fashioned way. He personally researched it.

There have been others who have personally raised the bar of environmental awareness. A partial roll call would include the following individuals:

Charles Darwin—born February 12, 1809, died April 19, 1882. A British naturalist, Darwin was the father of the theory of evolution. He wrote *The Origin of Species* in 1858, which when coupled with a contemporary's (Gregor Johann Mendel) findings, gave birth to the science of genetics. Perhaps Darwin's biggest environmental contribution was his findings that species exhibit niche and habitat selection. Conversely, it was realized that animal populations would die out in direct proportion to niche and habitat destruction. Darwin's theories, backed by analytical/statistical research, gave modern biology a boost and lifted it to the status of a science.

Henry David Thoreau—born July 12, 1817, died May 6, 1862. Thoreau, first and foremost a humanitarian, wrote his most well-known work *Walden* in 1854. *Walden* emphasizes a return to the simple life and a kinship with nature through keen observation and deep respect. This work has inspired and relaxed millions since its initial publication. A lesser-known yet scientifically significant essay entitled *Succession of Forest Trees* (1860) is considered by naturalists to be a major contribution to the literature.

Thoreau, always a peaceful man, did have a rebellious and righteous nature. In 1846 he refused to pay a poll tax in protest to American slavery and was jailed. Freed by an aunt who paid the tax for him, he shortly thereafter wrote *Civil Disobedience,* in which he encouraged readers to follow their hearts when they found the laws of the land unjust or inappropriate. This is certainly a code for the new ecologists to live by.

Frederick Law Olmsted—born April 26, 1822, died August 28, 1903. Olmsted is credited with being the father of landscape architecture, a profession which claims as its primary goal an ability to provide stewardship of the land so that it serves its highest and best purpose. Designer (with Calvert Vaux) of Central Park in New York City, Olmsted sought to bring the informal English garden style to many other public works. He was a champion for nature in the cities and preservation of the natural areas which laid beyond their fringes by being highly involved in the formation of Yosemite National Park in California.

John Muir—born April 21, 1838, died December 24, 1914. Born in Scotland, Muir immigrated to the United States in 1849. A staunch conservationist, Muir crusaded for national parks and wildlife reservations. His books and essays awakened a generation, most notably one Theodore Roosevelt, who, in 1908, named Muir Woods National Monument in Marin County, California after him in acknowledgement of his environmental achievements.

Theodore Roosevelt—born October 27, 1858, died

January 6, 1919. The twenty-sixth president of the United States, serving from 1901 to 1909, Roosevelt was a man of many talents and interests. A progressive, he dominated the political reform movement that had its heyday in the U.S. from 1900 to the start of World War I. An independent thinker and just as independent a leader, Roosevelt could always be counted on to stir things up. This goes for his legendary participation as leader of the Rough Riders in the Spanish American War (1898) to his trust busting of big business during his presidency to winning the Nobel Peace Prize to his forward-looking views on wildlife and habitat preservation.

Roosevelt enthusiastically backed Chief Forester Gifford Pinchot by increasing the holdings of the nation's forest reserve by millions of acres. He also was an avid supporter of conservation measures mandated on a state level. Roosevelt is generally considered the most environmentally sensitive and active U.S. president.

Franklin Delano Roosevelt –born January 30, 1882, died April 12, 1945. A distant relative to Teddy Roosevelt, FDR was the thirty-second president of the United States and served its longest term of twelve consecutive years (1933 to 1945). He died at the start of his fourth term, which would have had him serve an unprecedented sixteen years. Best remembered for pulling America out of the Great Depression era through programs created to service his initial campaign platform, whereby he promised the American public a "New Deal." Banking practices were revamped, home loans made easier to obtain, and farm credit made more widely available. In 1933, Roosevelt created the Civilian Conservation Corps (CCC) or "Job Corps," as the program became to be known. Perhaps the greatest single aid to conservation and the unemployed, at its height in 1935 there were twenty-six hundred

CCC camps employing five hundred thousand young men in resource conservation projects. The program was abolished in 1942, primarily because most able-bodied young men were conscripted into or volunteered for military service in World War II. There has never been a nature-based project like this in the U.S. before or after the New Deal. Although I must say, it certainly appears that the time is long overdue to reshuffle the deck.

Aldo Leopold—born January 11, 1887, died April 24, 1948. Leopold was a naturalist who advocated that undisturbed wilderness be set aside for all people to observe and enjoy, albeit from afar. His journal *A Sand County Almanac,* copyright 1949, inspired 1940s- and 1950s-era environmentalists who, in turn, inspired (or birthed) 1970s-era environmentalists. Arguably, the early 1970s could be referred to as the golden age of the environmental movement.

Rachel Carson—born May 27, 1907, died April 14, 1964. Most remembered for her landmark work *Silent Spring,* which describes the uncontrolled and indiscriminate use of pesticides. Carson's work spawned an entire generation of environmental activists. She is probably one of the most frequently attacked environmental authors, often being cited as an unrealistic purist. As recently as 1990 Dixy Lee Ray was taking potshots at her. Shame on you, Dixy. It's not good to speak ill of the dead. Carson earlier published *The Sea Around Us* (1951), which appeared on the U.S. nonfiction best-seller list for ten months and earned her the National Book Award. Whether you stand to the left or the right of the environmental movement, you would have to agree that without Rachel Carson it's highly likely that there wouldn't have been an environmental movement.

There are four ambassadors of ecological goodwill from my own profession, landscape architecture, that deserve an honorable mention. Garrett Eckbo wrote *The Landscape We See* in 1969. It served as an anthem for the profession for the next thirty years. Eckbo, always a visionary, predicted traffic gridlock and the importance of mitigating the effects of the freeway in the city. John Ormsbee Simonds has written *Landscape Architecture* and *Earthscape: A Manual of Environmental Planning.* The former defined the profession that most openly recognizes the need to provide stewardship of the land, and the latter raised serious questions as to the irresponsible nature with which we approach the built environment. Ian McHarg is perhaps the profession's most impassioned author. In his classic *Design with Nature* he is an avid proponent of development occurring in those areas of the Earth which are most capable of accommodating it. And finally, Eric Arthur Johnson, the voice of the Southwest, attempts through simply worded practical books (*The Low Water Flower Gardener* and *How to Grow Wildflowers in the Southwest*) to reach the layman or home gardener and advocate a policy of water conservation through responsible irrigation practices and the use of indigenous and arid region adapted plant materials. Thank you gentlemen, one and all. I'm honored to hold the same registration that you do, although I must admit I've done considerably less with it.

If any one of the individuals outlined above had believed that they couldn't have made a difference, if they had just gone (or would just go) quietly off to their deaths without attempting to be heard, then there would quite possibly be no need for this book or any others like it. Each action, each book, each crusade has a purpose, and quietly so too does *Environmental Cognizance.* I want to reach the man in the street, the everyday Joe, and tell him you can make a difference. First, by becoming better informed. Second, by taking some form of positive action no matter how small. And third, by truly believing that by your actions there *is hope for the future.*

But, it's a big world out there. Nobody knows for sure just how many Homo sapiens there are. Estimates range from 6 to 8 billion. Demographics is not an exact science. We live on an Earth of different peoples with dramatically different agendas. Some agendas are driven by the quest for fame and/or power, but most are driven by a desire for economic advancement. As an identifiable objective, nurturing the planet that sustains us comes in a distant third if it comes in at all. Sadly, the more things change the more they stay the same.

But in order to inherit the Earth, change is inevitable. There are so many of us that you would think that one new leader, one new free thinker, one new child of God might be able to rise up and show us all a solution to the global environmental problems. Yes, it's a big world out there and no one knows when or from where the next prophet will come, yet we all hope she/he will come soon. It's such a big world.

Into this fragmented, economically diverse world, a man is born. He is just one man with one life. How it will be lived depends on geography and the grace of God. One man—one life. Less than a hundred years to live it. A mere grain in the hourglass of time. One man—one life. One Earth on which to live it. One man—one life. One chance to get it right.

Life. Sweet life on Earth. To breathe, and walk, and be a part of it. To witness and enjoy the Earth. To live upon the land and put back more than you take. To learn from those that came before and pave the way for those to come. It is a blessing to understand the Earth and natural processes but, more importantly, to enjoy the thousands of little things. The slicing sound of wind that the wings of gliding ravens makes stirs the soul. Their gentle, severe cawing is their way of boasting that they are floating free while we are not. The ripple of fish in a pond. The full moon, warm rain, powder snow, and sunsets. The Earth is always with us. While we do our best to ignore it, she constantly reminds us of all things big, unstoppable, and misunderstood.

When will we know for sure that we will be able to save the planet and ourselves in the process? We are poised at the doorstep to the new millennium, and we have no idea how long it will take. We only know that if it takes much longer then it won't be necessary to worry about the survival of our species anymore. Time is of the essence, so we keep asking ourselves—*when?*

2010 is too optimistic, while 2020 is obtainable and convenient. I'll be sixty-eight in 2020. God willing, I could leave this Earth knowing she is quite capable of surviving and prospering in my absence. There's twenty-one years left to get the job done. There's a definite sense of urgency to accomplish something noteworthy in order to be remembered as a noteworthy man. One man—one life.

And not a lot of time is left in which to live it. One man—one life—on sweet planet Earth. At its best, could Heaven really be better than this? The land, the sky, and the water. One man—one life. I've been fortunate enough to know and love it all.

Part Two:

Composed circa 2002

Chapter Nine

The Newologists

It's been three long years since I last wrote anything in *Environmental Cognizance.* Originally, I felt that I had said all that I wanted to say as succinctly as I wanted to say it and that was that. Forty publisher rejection letters and some friendly reviewer advice has made me pick up the pen again. Aside from the publishers who just flat considered me an uninspiring writer, there was a thread of commonality in the criticism. Most had published similar books, or so they thought after a light scanning of mine. Others hit the nail more directly on the head when they responded that there was *nothing new* in my text. Most of what I said had been said elsewhere, could be found in other resources, particularly magazines, or had been amply documented in film. All one had to do was just look. This missed the point of my "reaching the man in the street" angle entirely. I didn't want him to go looking for environmental enlightenment, because I knew with the effort that that would take, he wouldn't. I wanted to write something fast, pointed, and thought provoking—provide a quick, state-of-the-art environmental primer, if you will. In other words, if the man in the street didn't seek the environmental message, I was going to hit him over the head with it. In reflection, I wonder if this is the crux of the environmental problem—that people are just too hardheaded to listen no matter how loud you shout. Well, so much for publishers.

One paid ($475.00) reviewer/agent stated that it was obvious that I was hurt and angry, but the buying public just wanted answers. Just eliminate chapters 1 and 2, tack on a few more, send it in with the $2,800 editorial fee, and we would be well on our way to literary representation with a class "A" publisher. What were the forty others? Class "B" publishers? I had to wonder if they had even read a word I had written or just drawn a conclusion from the insightful cover letter that was intended to get them frothing at the mouth to read on. I also had to wonder who, if they truly knew the breadth of the worldwide environmental calamity we find ourselves in, wouldn't be angry? Besides that, I am way beyond angry and dwell in a mindset of complete and utter disgust.

Then a nice letter from a Colorado publisher arrived. It read:

> *Dear Mr. Krieg:*
>
> *A number of our staff members have read your proposal,* Environmental Cognizance: Towards the Year 2020, *and it was very well received. We feel you have an intense message and most of us agree strongly with your viewpoints. However, due to the fact that we have several similar books that we will be publishing in the next few years, we must decline publication. We wish you luck finding a publisher for this important book.*

Geniuses, pure geniuses all of them. And God bless them

all. It's truly amazing what mountains a tiny grain of encouragement can move. It got me writing again. By damn, I wasn't angry after all. I was just *intense*. And, on top of that, if they want something new, then I'll give them new. Which brings us to the newest of the new—the Newologists.

They come from all walks of life; gender, color, and physical appearance doesn't matter a bit. They may or may not be smart. But they sure are dedicated. This is key, believe me, for to get to the bottom of things the Newologists are going to have to work morning, noon, and night.

First on our list is the new breed of environmental writers trying to explain nature, natural processes, and the breadth of the environmental issue in terms that we can all understand. The aforementioned David Quammen would top this list. An advocate of Edward Abbey, who was ahead of his time as an intellect and perhaps behind it as a redneck, Quammen entertains us with a lively intellect that's tongue-in-cheek. I don't know of anyone else who could hold my attention during dissertations on mosquitoes and black widow spiders. After riveting our attention with zany commentary, he slips in more serious environmental issues such as species population dynamics and the diversity of their gene pool as it relates to impending extinction. Quammen clearly loves nature and all things natural, but even he had to be a realist when writing about a species teetering on the brink of extinction and about to fall into the abyss. In *Song of the Dodo* he states:

> *And hopeless cases waste money. And money is a limiting factor, of course, in the design and implementation of conservation efforts. There just isn't enough cash to deliver a program of individualized rescue to every endangered species of bird, reptile, mammal, insect and plant . . .* [5]

David Brower, the first executive director of the Sierra

Club who served for a period spanning thirty years, offers up a brilliant little manual titled *Let the Mountains Talk, Let the Rivers Run.* While offering the sage advice that an eighty-eight-year lifetime can bring, he stands staunchly on one point—the environment must be continuously fought for. States Brower:

> *What has happened to boldness in defense of the Earth? For all the splendid increases in membership of the world's environmental organizations, both wilderness and the ecological life—support systems for the planet itself are increasingly going down the tubes . . . Too often, in the 1990s environmentalists are so eager to appear reasonable that they have gone soft.* [6]

Michael Pollan, in *The Botany of Desire,* explores four types of cash crops (apple, tulip, marijuana, and potato) in an effort to illustrate that botanical history had an effect on and is furthered by the present. In an interesting twist, he poses the question of whether we domesticated certain plants for our use or did certain plants allow us to domesticate them to assure their own survival? I find most interesting his premise that all the brilliant young botanical minds are in hiding in the underground world of indoor marijuana cultivation. Could be. You never know. Equally as revealing are the advances in genetic engineering that are either producing beneficial plants or landing us at the door step of Armageddon—take your pick.

Pollan fears developing a species that is not necessarily hideous but for which we have no defenses if it decides it wants more than we intended it to have. He states:

> *Jumping genes and superweeds point to a new kind of environmental problem, "biological pollution," which*

some environmentalists believe will be the unhappy legacy of agriculture's shift from a chemical to a biological paradigm. (We're already familiar with one form of biological pollution: invasive exotic species such as kudzu, zebra mussels, and Dutch elm disease.) Harmful as chemical pollution can be, it eventually disperses and fades, but biological pollution is self-replicating. Think of it as the difference between an oil spill and a disease. Once a transgene introduces a new weed or a resistant pest into the environment, it can't very well be cleaned up: it will already have become part of nature. [7]

Recently there's been a movement in genetic engineering circles that wants to reintroduce extinct species, the most notable example being *Thylacinus cynacephaolus*, a rare marsupial wolf from Tasmania, or the once commonly known Tasmanian Tiger. Refer to Quammen's *Song of the Dodo* for an elaboration of how bounty hunters supported by sheepherders blasted this creature into oblivion at the turn of the twentieth century. Now, from a fetus pickled in formaldehyde in a near-century-old glass jar, scientists perhaps one step removed from Dr. Frankenstein want to bring it back into existence. I question the credibility of genetically reengineering species that were vehemently detested or couldn't compete back then, when conditions would be worse for them now. In other words, I think we should spend available funding on the future and not the past.

In *Buffalo for the Broken Heart,* Dan O'Brien shares his trials as a cattle rancher near the Black Hills of South Dakota. With cattle ranching leading him to financial collapse, due to the fact that these ungulates are ill suited to the rigors of the land he tries to raise them on, O'Brien opts to convert his operation to managing a buffalo herd. It's a simple concept of returning a creature that is ideally suited to the land back to its indigenous habitat. Writer O'Brien states:

> *And that is when I figured out the problem with cows. It's not that there is anything wrong with them in general. It's just that out here on the Great Plains, they seem painted on the landscape in a way that will never allow them to be truly part of it. They have always been a sort of ungulate tourist, and in ranching them I felt a little like a tour guide who spends his life translating menus and pointing out the restrooms. Sometime after that, I started thinking about that buffalo I'd seen in the road. He was no tourist and no one's ward, and in a land as hard as mine, nothing is more valuable.* [8]

Quammen started his writing career by trying to carve out a living in standard literature. As an assistant to no less a literary figure than William Faulkner, he eventually grew tired of fiction and turned his efforts towards nature writing. Brower was a major in the mountain patrol during World War II and a mountaineer of some notoriety after it. He simply loved to be outdoors. Pollan loves gardening and writing and has found a way to merge the two. O'Brien started out a wildlife biologist, then turned to raising and hunting with peregrine falcons before acquiring a ranch in South Dakota on which to raise cattle and mellow out. His experience in trying to reestablish peregrines back into their natural habitat opened his stream of consciousness to habitat restoration in general. He knew and loved birds, then grew to love habitat, and then grew to revere the rightful inhabitants of that habitat.

Most of these men did not start out a biologist, a scientist, an ecologist. They came to environmentally enhanced lifestyles because these careers seemed to have found them. Their most telling thread of commonality is that they were drawn to nature to the point of crafting wonderfully written environmentally slanted literature. In a similar fashion, this is what the Newologist does. He somehow finds a way to become involved in the environmental movement. Any one of them may have come to their careers in a roundabout way, but once instilled with the responsibility of protecting nature it became their passion. That's where the Trainedologist and Newologist part company. One makes his work a living, and the other lives for his work. What I admire most is that they're out there doing it any way they can, not knowing if they will make a difference with the public at large, but, hopefully, content with the difference they have made with themselves.

Next up for recognition as Newologists are city and regional planners, for as we shall see in the next chapter, the best way to preserve wild areas is to stay out of them, and the only way we are going to do that is to be satisfied with where we are currently at.

I used to look at planners as having their heads so far out in the future that anything that they might actually come up with would be virtually meaningless. Now, with the passage of time and the wisdom that aging forces upon us, I realize that they have a place in the grand scheme of things, for someone must be out there riding the point in order for the platoon to march forward.

Planners and the zoning ordinances they create (or boilerplate perpetuate) mold the built landscape. The only way the creeping crud of suburbia or typical, along-the-highway countryside development is going to change from its moronic, rigid ways is to rewrite the codes. The easiest way to do this is to impress upon the planners how our lives really function, how we feel secure, how we perceive space, and what we would like to have left behind for our families after we pass on.

Any form of planning relies on accurate input in order to make informed decisions or policies. Garbage in means garbage out, and this is apparently what has been happening since the seventies, as garbage surrounds us. Did the ability to think creatively die with Woodstock or a few years later when most of the babies of the baby boomers graduated college? Boy did we ever get knocked around then, when we traded in peace and love for a tract home and a paycheck.

Dolores Hayden, in her marvelous book *Redesigning the American Dream,* suggests that we have no idea of who we really are. Nowhere does this fact manifest itself more than in the construction and consumption of the single-family home. Hayden writes:

> *The United States is a society of diverse cultures and household types, yet since the 1940s, most American space has been shaped around a simplistic prescription for satisfaction. Cities and housing have been designed to satisfy a nation of white, young, nuclear families, with father as breadwinner, mother as housewife, and children reared to emulate these same limited roles. While prescriptive literature in the form of sermons, housekeeping guides, and etiquette manuals has always been available to define the ideal middle-class Christian family, our post-World War II cities mark the triumph of a prescriptive architecture of gender on a national scale. A nation of homes tied to the mid-nineteenth-century ideal of separate spheres for women and men was something fanatical Victorian moralists only dreamed about, a utopia of male-female segregation they never expected the twentieth century to build. While maxims about true womanhood and manly dominance were the staple of Christian bourgeois Victorian culture in the United States, England, and many other*

countries, only in the United States in the twentieth century were so many material resources committed to reinforcing these ideas by spatial design.

In 2002, only a tiny percentage of American families include a male breadwinner, a unemployed housewife, and children under eighteen. The valiant World War II heroes and their blushing brides have now retired. About a quarter of all households are married couples with children under eighteen, but the father is the sole breadwinner in only 29.2 percent of those families. The predominant family type is the two-earner family. The fastest growing family type is the single-parent family, and five out of six single parent households are headed by women. Over a quarter of all households consist of one person living alone, be they young singles or the elderly. [9]

When we can grasp who we truly are we will finally be free from the shackles of unchecked consumption. Homes can become smaller by virtue of the fact that we don't have to put so many people in them. They can be located closer to urban centers, freeing owners of commuter time and costs. And they can definitely be more attractive if we can accept the fact that bigger is not better. Better is better.

How housing relates to city, town, and village centers also falls on the originality or lack thereof of the zoning codes. The same can be said for commercial and industrial development. John Ormshee Simonds proposed more thoughtful layouts way back in 1978 when he wrote *Earthscape* and championed Planned Community Development:

Until recently, as noted, the customary procedure in community planning has been to subdivide a larger property into strips or parcels fronting upon both sides of all public streets. Homes or other buildings have been "shoe-

horned" onto the lots on the basis of mandatory setbacks from each property line. Further restrictions have usually been imposed in the form of minimum lot sizes; height limitations; general positioning of driveways, parking bays, and garages; and the prohibition of screening hedges or freestanding privacy walls.

These outmoded practices have encouraged developers to clear and level all possible areas of the site and to fit the maximum number of structures within the prescribed building limits. It has resulted in streets which are hazardous and inefficient. Homes and family life are faced upon busy thoroughfares instead of quiet courts or recreation spaces. Prodigious amounts of land are wasted in unusable side yards and often front yards which are neither quiet nor conducive to out-of-door living, and many communities have lost all contact with unspoiled nature.

Planned Community Development, a fresh approach to land planning, has been made possible in many localities through the adoption of a PCD amendment. [10]

Apparently where I live is not one of these many localities.

Perhaps the most distressing thing that current zoning ordinances spawn is a homogenization and separation of all but the most similar of land uses. This is what provides variety in some of the more memorable cities around the world and what we miss the most when we wax nostalgic about what was good about small towns in the good old days.

The heart has been cut out of our city and village centers, schools have been banished to the edge of town, and once quaint shopping districts have been interned to the regional mall. Any place that cannot be reached by automobile is apparently not worth going to, and anyone who doesn't own a car is apparently a hopeless loser.

But it is we who have really lost. The inflexible zoning ordinances force us to be simplistic humanoids who drive from one prescribed-use area to another. Our lives are a succession of wrapped boxes only to be unwrapped on an as-needed basis. We no longer have the richness of a vibrant community at our fingertips and within walking distance. While traveling incessantly in our cars we are in minimum security prison, and when we arrive home we check into maximum security prison.

The planners finally have a recognizable challenge, which is to spring society from its self-inflicted incarceration and let it roam uninhibited and free upon the land. These Newologists can bring nature back to the city and the observation of natural processes back to our lives.

The third wave of Newologists come from a segment of our population that one would least expect. Hunters and fishermen frequently spend more time outdoors than the typical outdoor writer. Teddy Roosevelt, after all, simply wanted natural spaces preserved because the species that he hunted lived there. He wanted to assure himself a never-ending and self-replenishing supply of game. Any port in a storm, I say.

Those that extract from the land are the ones who should pay the most for the use of it. I'm not for gun control, but I am for hunter control. I feel that if individuals are allowed to go out and trample the landscape then they should know something about it. Similar to testing for a driving permit/license, I feel hunters and fishermen should be exposed to environmental instruction and testing and subject to ongoing *renewals* of such. In other words, they should pay more and definitely know more, for once imbued with this knowledge of the land, they may well come to acquire a deep and abiding respect for it. What an irony to think that the dreaded and frequently chastised hunter/fisherman may become a better naturalist than the armchair naturalists if for no other reason than they are out interacting responsibly with nature.

And finally, the newest of the new Newologists. You and me, brother, and possibly the man in the street. We can't count on the government, because Clinton/Gore, who were this generation's best shot at meaningful environmental legislation, are gone. Seems that former President Clinton concentrated more on his mounting loins than mountain lions. I've said it before—we can't count on the scientists, for they are far too concerned with quantifying the breadth of the problem rather than doing anything, no matter how small, to attack it head-on.

The Newologists, one and all, are collectively going to define their role as participants in the environmental movement. They are going to do this in a manner revolutionary to the established mores of the existing scientific community.

In short, *they are simply going to do something.*

Chapter Ten

A Sustainable America

As a landscape architect in a desert region, for over twenty-five years I've become intimately familiar with the emotional, physical, and environmental power of an oasis. Our American cities should be oases where mind and body are nurtured, where the visitor is delighted, indeed feels fortunate, to be there. This is the concentrated celebration of mankind and our supposedly civilized society. It is also where we fail the most.

American development patterns usually have well-defined lines between cities, countryside, natural areas, and truly wild places. Ninety percent of any given lifetime is spent within one of the first three areas while longing for wilderness. For this reason, the thrust of this chapter will be to examine improving and sustaining land that is privately held, for while we clamor for the government to protect our wild lands, who protects and enhances those areas where we predominately live? In my first book, *Desert Landscape Architecture,* I referred to these three main areas as the "oasis, transition, feather to desert theory," which I explained thusly:

> *This theory originates by just studying the pattern of human habitation in any desert region. Humans settle in an area with a dependable supply of water and plant gardens for enjoyment*—the oasis. *They simultaneously plant agricultural fields and groves of trees for survival purposes. Indigenous vegetation invades at the periphery of the agricultural zone utilizing the more abundant soil moisture*—the transition. *In varying degrees, the density of the native vegetation decreases as the terrain moves away from the human development until conditions are the same as they always were*—feather to desert.
>
> *Applying this theory to landscape architectural design is easy and beneficial. Planting around the building is relatively thick. Plant material selection, while responding to microclimate, is greener, and its moisture content cools the ground plane and/or provides shade to the structure*—the oasis.
>
> *Planting that extends out into other use areas thins, while plant species selection is towards less water demanding to near drought tolerant*—the transition. *Hydroseed mixes for seasonal color, thicker than normal native cactus plantings, and eventually raw desert occurs as you fade farther away from the building*—feather to desert.

While more pronounced and prevalent in desert regions, this pattern of development has manifested itself time and time again in the American landscape from the Atlantic shore to the Pacific coast. Our first battle in building a sustainable America should be fought in the reexamination of the uses and layouts of our American cities, which former President Lyndon Johnson stated were the end products of "stupidity and greed." As ugly as they got, cities could always be improved upon through the introduction of nature and natural processes. Where would New York be without Olmsted's Central Park? What did the river walk do for San Antonio? San Diego's zoo is world renowned and draws revenues that aid wildlife research around the globe.

Although it may initially seem like a gigantic compromise, Americans have to consider the environmental middle ground. A host of environmental writers are certainly right that the home-in-the-country syndrome is a major contributor to loss of habitat, especially for those truly wild species who weren't country before country was cool. A simple objective for preserving wild places would be to bring the country to cities and suburbs so the fresh air mongers would stay put. Easier said than done.

New parks, museums, green spaces, and privately held mini-wildlife preserves could bring nature back to the city so that people could connect to it if only on a subliminal level. Infill of vacant urban lots, street trees, park expansions, and the like will always make cities more attractive. A reordering of suburban areas so that houses don't look like cracker boxes all in a row is long overdue.

Tony Hiss, in *The Experience of Place,* examines how cities *live and feel* as a more important premise than how they look, which is good, because most of them look terrible. Then he, perhaps more than any other author, examines the transition between city and countryside only to determine that these areas are in fact "working landscapes" with a beauty all their own. For lack of a better description, think of a Christmas card, calendar, or picture postcard of rural New England. Hiss wants to preserve it. Groups have been formed to save the barns of Vermont, the agricultural areas of New Hampshire, the Amish countryside of rural Pennsylvania. Apparently man's imprint upon the landscape hasn't been all bad, and given the time to evolve, American landscapes have a credible visual history. The problem is that time is compressed, as population pressures do not allow for an evolution into romantic scenic countryside. First, we must preserve and protect what is left, and second, we must develop methodologies for establishing livable transition zones between city and countryside and countryside and natural areas.

A sustainable America depends on a three-pronged program of revitalizing cities, thoroughly planning and limiting expansion into the countryside, and keeping natural areas natural. The major problem is clearly defining which area is which, especially in light of our second goal, which is to blur the transition lines between the three zones so as to make the visual landscape seamless. This goal of a seamless landscape assumes a cooperation between species and, more importantly, a cooperative effort between the environmentalists and the rest of mankind.

Ian McHarg, in *Design with Nature,* took the lead in establishing a policy whereby nature and mankind could coexist. Written in the early seventies, the public at large was not yet ready to embrace the concept. Now, thirty years later, we are not only ready to accept the concept as truth but have written environmental protection into our laws and indelibly across our collective national consciousness. While many landscape architects, some urban and land planners, and a handful of politicians are enlightened, the public, for the most part, remains clueless as to how to approach a sustainable America. More than this even, who is to determine what an acceptable level of sustainability is?

While there are various levels of environmental purity,

there is only one Earth. The biologists, ecologists, and naturalists want to preserve what's left of it. I, as a landscape architect, want to improve upon what has already been built in hopes that nature can be reintroduced into the populous areas. Here landscape design is an interpretation more than an emulation of natural processes. A tree in the city is worth its weight in gold not only because of its inherent beauty but also because it connects mankind to the greater environment beyond the city limit signs.

Population will continue to grow and cities will sprawl if left to their historical devices. Unchecked expansion into natural areas will lead to eventual environmental collapse. It's a matter of apathetic acceptance, but even more than that, it's a consequence of gross inaction. *But action must be taken if we are to sustain ourselves.*

If there is a goal to preserve natural places then there should be an even larger goal to improve and enhance that which has already been constructed. By achieving the environmental middle ground one can establish a jumping-off point for perpetuating the wild places that comprise the higher ground.

In his classic *The Geography of Nowhere,* James Howard Kunstler traces the dismantling of American cities by that twentieth-century culprit of culprits—the automobile. Cities were bisected, dissected, and eventually spit out the tailpipe as the runaway car sped towards the suburbs and points beyond, leaving decimated neighborhoods and abandoned downtowns in its wake. Those who were left behind had committed that most hideous of American sins—they couldn't afford a car. Without transportation they had to stay close to urban centers for goods and services. Then the urban centers began to crumble from the inside out. They became a magnet for the homeless, unemployed, and poverty-stricken masses. Landlords stopped maintaining buildings, while tenants stopped maintaining any quality of life.

The car culture fled faster and farther from the cities. People fled to the suburbs, which proved to be worse than the cities, and those that could fled to the country. Now what was city/suburb became city, and what was suburb/country became suburb. The lowest common denominator prevailed as the lower desirable area of human habitation sucked up the next highest one. In terms of lifestyles, the minimum became the maximum. Life is always perceived as being better at the outer edge, so, like giant amoebas, cities bloat outward. Longer distances exert pressures on utility and transportation systems. Automotive purchases and maintenance costs escalate to the point where they preclude owning a home, which was the primary reason for moving away from the city in the first place.

The cycle now complete, the resigned suburbanites watch their Direct TV's, dreaming of a home in the country, while the country dwellers watch their fence lines, praying against further intrusion from the suburbs. Those who love nature and natural areas watch with horror as president George Bush II appoints Gale Norton secretary of the interior and wonder how long it will be before developers devise land lease programs for housing on public land. If oil and timber interests can do it, why not them? Countryside/natural areas become countryside? Where do we draw the line? Without reservation, at the countryside. And how do we do that? By making the built landscape so appealing that people will gladly want to stay there. Now, herein lies the problem. Beauty costs money, and while certainly appreciated when it's for free, it's something that people will decide to do without when faced with a bill. The upper class, when faced with footing everyone else's bill to clean up and preserve the countryside, will opt to live in the currently uncluttered natural areas. What's the difference between countryside and natural areas? A road, a house, a septic system—*a neighbor.*

Rather than growing from the inside out, America has to promote growth from the outside in. Our lives, like our transportation systems, have to reverse themselves. America moved first by waterway, then by rail, then by highways and airplanes. As fossil fuels deplete, mass transit systems will experience a resurgence. People will strive to get closer to their workplace. Imagine an exodus not farther out but deeper in.

Why is the human habitation cycle any different than any other cycle? When cycles reach their defined limits they close upon themselves. What's key to a sustainable America is to say *this is the limit.* If countryside is all that's left to develop, then we had better put some real thought into how it will eventually look.

Alison Hawthorne Deming, in *The Edges of the Civilized World,* laments the huge country home occupied by a retired couple apparently longing for guests. She champions homes (if they must occur) of much less square footage in opposition to typical high-end country club home builders who routinely specify in their standards that homes must be five thousand or more square feet in size. This dictates more site usage for the home itself but also frequently triggers a "bigger is more beautiful" mentality as entry courts, patios, pools, everything increases in size to stay in scale with the behemoth house. Then there are the not-so-obvious drawbacks that you usually don't think about. Larger homes consume more natural resources inherent in the materials that comprise the large square footage. Energy consumption increases to the point of wastefulness in trying to heat and cool the plenteous interior rooms.

The only way to preserve existing habitat in the country is not to build on it. The only way to restore country within a built area is to reintroduce habitat. Those species most capable of coexistence are the ones most likely to survive into the next millennium. In this renovated country, fences have to go, and wildlife/migration corridors must be respected. Linear, along-the-highway-type development needs to be abandoned in lieu of a concentric village center with *parking in the rear.* Americans need to take back their lives from their cars. Once we do that, perhaps we may feel it's safe to go outside again.

Cities need to be made to live up to their promise as great gathering places, cultural centers, vibrant elaborate entertainment facilities, showplaces for the arts and educational advancement. When we can make going to the city an uplifting experience as opposed to a life-threatening one, then we can begin to contain and sustain a contented American populace. Our society has developed a myriad of medical and health devices to prolong life. Now we need to examine what it is that would make a longer life worth living.

As previously stated, the responsibility of my profession, landscape architecture, is to administer "stewardship of the land so that it serves its highest and best purpose." It's an egocentric goal and one that assumes that man is better suited than nature to determine what life should exist where. Human population growth and housing expansion has overwhelmed Mother Nature. While it would be nice to sit around and wait for an answer because "mother knows best," we are way past that point. We do have the benefit of experience in knowing what isn't working. We can still refer to what has worked in the past. We need more than anything else to remember that *there is only one Earth to work with.*

Let's clean up the mess that we have made of our cities, lessen expansion into the countryside, and try to leave natural areas alone. Let's work with what we already have to the fullest extent possible before grasping for more. Sustainability goes hand in hand with accountability. Rather than moving out farther while running away from our past mistakes, let's admit our errors and correct them.

Environmental purity exists in truly wild places that are off-limits to human expansion—we don't. The only way wild places will remain wild is to *leave them alone.* The only way developed places can become more wild is *to make them that way.* Let's reintroduce nature in the heart of the city. Let's leave the country in the countryside. Let's leave the wild places wild.

Let's improve our lives by improving our immediate surroundings. The environment should start at your fingertips, wherever they may reach. Beauty should be all around you, not something that has to be traveled to.

When Americans can truly be happy with the surroundings they occupy at all times, then we will have achieved a sustainable America from sea to shining sea.

Chapter Eleven

Saving the Planet

September 11, 2001. How can we even talk about saving the planet when monsters like this exist in the world? As a Christian, I've often wondered what difference it makes what happens to the Earth if our final destination is really Heaven? If life on Earth is a testing ground to determine eligibility for admittance into the afterlife, wouldn't it be enough to simply pray hard, live clean, and wait around to die?

Were we not instructed in Genesis to go forth and subdue the Earth? Have we not done a commendable job in accomplishing that? No. No because we have missed the point of subdue, or more fittingly, we fail to realize the difference between subdue and destroy.

We are stewards of the land whether we recognize that fact or not, if for no other reason than we exist upon it. As stewards we are expected not just to extract from it but to devise ways to multiply its bounty. Most environmentalists promote one disturbing point: that the population of the Earth, as it now exists, far exceeds the planet's carrying capacity. Like overdrafting of groundwater resources in an agricultural area, the problem is out of sight and out of mind until the aquifer runs dry. Then the farmer moves on until there is nowhere else to move to. Then what? To borrow an analogy from David Brower, consider the man who jumps from a sixty-story building. Plummeting through the air he says, "So good so far" when he's forty stories down.

The concept of stewardship is biblical. Quoting no less an authority than Jesus Christ in a parable from the book of Luke, we read:

> *A nobleman living in a certain province was called away to the distant capital of the empire to be crowned king of his province. Before he left he called together his assistants and gave them each $2,000 to invest while he was gone. Upon his return he called in the men to whom he had given the money to find out what they had done with it and what their profits were.*
>
> *The first man reported a tremendous gain—ten times as much as the original amount!*
>
> *"Fine!" the king exclaimed. "You are a good man. You have been faithful with the little I entrusted to you, and as your reward, you shall be governor of ten cities."*
>
> *The next man also reported a splendid gain—five times the original amount.*
>
> *"All right!" his master said. "You can be governor over five cities."*
>
> *But the third man brought back only the money he had started with. "I've kept it safe," he said, "because I was afraid (you would demand my profits), for you are a hard man to deal with, taking what isn't yours and even confiscating the crops that others plant."*
>
> *"You vile and wicked slave," the king roared. "Hard,*

am I? That's exactly how I'll be toward you! If you knew so much about me and how tough I am, then why didn't you deposit the money in the bank so that I could at least get some interest on it?"

Then, turning to the others standing by, he ordered, "Take the money away from him and give it to the man who earned the most."

"But sir," they said, "he has enough already!"

"Yes," the king replied, "but it is always true that those who have, get more, and those who have little, soon lose even that."

As we draw down the resources of the Earth and expand our ecological debt ratio, will this be our fate? As more is lost will the rate at which we are losing it be accelerated?

Our situation is worse than the man's in the Bible who did nothing. He didn't necessarily lose a thing. He just didn't gain anything. Because the world's resources are in a position of deficit we must not only slow the negative flow but increase interest-bearing investments such as habitat restoration just to get the world's environmental bank account back to even.

Slowing the negative flow requires reducing the demand, which of course means stabilizing and then reducing world population. This may already be happening if you believe Peter Huber from *Hard Green,* who writes:

For the planet as a whole, population continues to rise, because of the several-generation lags between fertility and mortality changes on the one hand and population changes on the other. World population was 1.6 billion at the beginning of the century and 2.5 billion in 1950. It is about 6 billion at the end of the century and is projected to reach somewhere between 7.5 and 9.4 billion by 2050. Then it will start shrinking. Down to about 6 billion in

2100 and 4.3 billion in 2150, according to long-range UN projections. As Wattenberg notes, a bust, like an explosion, moves in a geometric progression. [11]

What's clear is that for the short term, say the life spans of our current grandchildren, things are bound to get much worse. Then as population decreases, things could possibly get better if (and it's a big if) there's anything left to work with. In other words, what we do today will most likely have the greatest effect on the lives of our great, great grandchildren. To work selflessly towards the goal of a better tomorrow three generations removed from our own is truly a noble goal. The only question is, *are we really that selfless?*

To understand the importance of keeping the Earth life forces in balance and why mankind is incredibly fortunate to have the Earth, one has no further to look than the Gaia Hypothesis. In 1968 James E. Lovelock and Lynn Margulis proposed the Gaia Hypothesis, which credited microbial life as the true developers of the Earth, particularly its atmosphere. Gaia was able to explain why we are fortunate enough to have an atmosphere at all. Our air is comprised predominately of nitrogen (77 percent) and oxygen (21 percent), two chemicals that react explosively when in contact with each other on the other planets. The buffer, stabilizer, peace negotiator between the two gases appears to be the remaining 2 percent of trace gases, of which carbon dioxide used to comprise roughly 1 percent. But now comes the culprit, carbon dioxide, spewing forth as a by-product of the gasoline engines of the world and upsetting the precious atmospheric apple cart.

Bill McKibben, in *The End of Nature,* writes:

So—we have increased the amount of carbon dioxide in the air by about 25 percent in the last century and will almost certainly double it in the next; we have more than

> *doubled the level of methane; we have added a soup of other gases.* We have substantially altered the Earth's atmosphere.
>
> *This is not like local pollution, not like smog over Los Angeles. This is the Earth's entire atmosphere. If you'd climbed some remote mountain in 1960 and sealed up a bottle of air at its peak and did the same thing this year, the two samples would be substantially different. Their basic chemistry would have changed. Most discussions of the greenhouse gases rush immediately to their future consequences—is the sea going to rise?—without pausing to let the simple fact of what has already happened sink in. The air around us, even where it is clean and smells like spring and is filled with birds, is* different, *significantly changed . . .*
>
> *And the result, when increased carbon dioxide and other trace gases are taken as givens, does not differ all that much from what Arrhenius forecast.* The models that have been constructed agree that when, as has been predicted, the level of carbon dioxide or its equivalent in other greenhouse gases doubles from pre-Industrial Revolution concentrations, the global average temperature will increase, and that the increase will be 1.5 to 4.5 degrees celsius, or 3 to 8 degrees fahrenheit. [12]

It's utterly amazing what altering a few percentage points in atmospheric gaseous content or a few degrees in global temperatures will do to shake up life on Earth. Seems like that playful lady Gaia, so named after a Greek goddess, will be needed more than ever. In other words, we need to preserve microbial life and plant evergreen trees to suck up carbon dioxide. Either that or Miami will be underwater and the Great Plains a dust bowl. As absurd as it seems, we must remember that those melting ice caps are comprised of *fresh water*. This is water that could be transported, although at huge expense, to the thirsty parts of the world.

Gaia does bring to light the important scientific principle that living things affect chemical and physical processes occurring around them. In the case of our Earth, this phenomenon eventually made the planet conducive to human habitation. By supporting Gaia we support ourselves, and by disrupting Gaia we endanger ourselves. Let's treat Gaia like a lady.

Hand in hand with clean air comes clean water, for we can't survive without it. Think in terms of the two P's—preservation and purification. Preservation, while certainly pertaining to protecting underground water tables, in larger part should focus on preventing misuse and waste. Alternate sources of water treatment, particularly increased use of gray water to irrigate crops and domestic landscapes, need to be further explored and employed. The point here is to use only the pure water that is absolutely essential for survival. Water purification by utilizing several more layers of filtration as opposed to chemical treatment will undoubtedly increase the costs of potable water, but perhaps these costs will be offset by decreased costs of health care and disease prevention.

If you think of the surface of the Earth as being the approximate size of a handheld cell phone, then the amount of fresh water would be the size of one of the buttons on the key pad. Of all the water on Earth, only 3 percent of it is fresh. You can look at this one of two ways. First, that the oceans must be extremely vast, or second, that the amount of fresh water is extremely limited. Desalination of ocean water has proved doable but roughly as expensive as towing icebergs down from the Arctic. Clearly, water conservation is the order of the day.

With air to breathe and water to drink, man now needs food to survive at all and shelter to survive comfortably. The world's current supply of mass-produced agricultural food relies on the monocultural planting of grains, vegetables, fruits, nuts, and berries. These plantings are made to produce at maximum levels through applications of massive dosages of chemical fertilizers. Harvesting employs fleets of fossil fuel dependent machinery, while distribution likewise relies on a fossil fuel dependent trucking system.

In the not-too-distant future, as fossil fuel reserves deplete, we will have to rely more on point-of-origin food production. Monocultural acreages will need to be diversified, as foods from a specific region will have to stay in that region. We won't have the same variety of foods, although we will probably have enough quantity.

Organic farming has proven cost prohibitive to date. A hybrid system that employs mass composting and the by-products of regional sewage treatment facilities will most likely provide enough nutrient-rich soil amendments, which when coupled with crop-rotation strategies, will allow a production level that assures an acceptable level of production if not an abundance.

America should return the buffalo to the plains because they are more efficient consumers of our native grasslands than cattle. This one change in our national diet could serve to feed more of the peoples that comprise the worldwide diet. Other nations should examine historic food sources indigenous to their land. Any edible species capable of living off the land as it exists rather than how it is enhanced will prove to be a boon to resource preservation.

Shelter—housing the burgeoning world population in a world of vanishing building materials is a daunting task. Our forests, what is left of them, can be looked at as being somewhat renewable within the constraints of a fifteen- to twenty-year rotation. Each successive cut yields poorer quality timber, which is, of course, a concern. And one has to wonder, if trees are the major absorbers of rampant carbon dioxide emissions then why are we cutting them at all? Alternative building materials are constantly being researched, but to date, they represent a very small part of the resources consumed by the building industry. Homes of *smaller square footage* across the board is the quickest way to stretch existing building materials. We may need our space, but when inclement weather arrives we need a roof over our heads even more.

Dolores Hayden, in *Redesigning the American Dream,* condensed piles of architectural literature and theory down to the three basic notions of roof, fire, and center. States Hayden:

> *The house forms of tribal societies dazzle the world traveler with ingenious responses to the challenge of building for various sites, climates, and household types. Jungle houses on stilts near the upper Amazon, three-story adobe complexes of the Pueblos in New Mexico, white-rimmed cave dwellings of the fishermen of southern Morocco, tall windscoop houses of Hyderabad in India, dark, arching Bedouin tents, turf-insulated Mongolian yurts—all are the work of skillful builders. The women and men who constructed them exploited the potential of sun and wind and made maximum use of reeds, ice, mud, rock, clay, goat hair, or grass. House forms reveal the varied marriage and kinship patterns of pre-industrial societies. The longhouses of the Iroquois accommodate many firesides consisting of a woman and her children. The circular dwellings of the Hakka represent an Asian communal tradition. The painted tepees of the Kiowa communicate hierarchies in a*

nomadic culture. The compounds of the Yoruba enclose the patriarchal lineage. The high thresholds of the Han courtyards keep evil spirits and strangers from joining the extended family. The high-walled houses and carved doors of Muslim Lamu enforce purdah, the traditional seclusion of women. Each of these designs encompasses a web of economic arrangements: through the organization of space they reinforce people's relationships to land, tools, rooms, animals, fire, food, and each other.

Vernacular house forms are economic diagrams of the reproduction of the human race. They are also aesthetic essays on the meaning of life within a particular culture, its joys and travails, its superstitions and stigmas. House forms cannot be separated from their physical and social contexts . . .

In industrial societies, humans retain a strong desire to own a piece of land, a house, and meaningful household objects in order to communicate, to themselves and to others, just who they are and how they wish to be treated . . .

The design and production of most residential space in the United States is handled by speculative developers, although sometimes developers hire architects to help them make aesthetic decisions. As a result of treating housing space as a commodity, residents' uncertainty about the meaning of roof, fire, and center is profound—as profound as the ambivalence about home, mom, and apple pie. The transition from vernacular house forms to modern housing has left everyone, architects included, confused about styles, periods, places, and cultural symbols. The aesthetic confusion and the familial confusion compound each other, and neither can be unraveled without the other. [9]

Translated, this means that homes were much better suited to their physical and cultural surroundings when they simply responded to the primeval needs for shelter and the constraints imposed by indigenous building materials (form follows function). Once affluence and opinions about style got thrown into the mix, any number of gaudy, flamboyant, ridiculous, inefficient, and stupid structures followed.

Renowned landscape architects Thomas Church and Garrett Eckbo (among others) started to extend the boxed house outward in the early fifties by introducing the outdoor room concept that the rest of the profession (those who were paying attention, anyways) referred to as the "California Style." Here, house and garden merged to create a living experience within a self-contained envelope of land, and nothing was more important then the transition zone between indoor and outdoor space. It was the heyday of the profession, which showed huge promise in that homeowners were enthusiastic about utilizing their land/home in a way that served its highest and best purpose. This renaissance was short lived.

By the sixties, the baby boomers had pumped out enough babies to necessitate a wasteland of suburban growth at the fringes of every American city. Who had time for gardening? With a stay-at-home wife and four kids to support, beleaguered dads commuted to their dead-end jobs in the cities in their fossil fuel guzzling chariots of Detroit steel. Families became so unhappy that they anesthetized themselves with television, rock and roll, divorce, and silly meaningless dances such as the twist. Lost in this societal upheaval was that the face of suburbia was steadily growing worse. Housing became little cracker boxes all in a row.

In the seventies some forward-thinking architects and planners started to notice the creeping crude emanating like shock waves from the cities out into the countryside and took action to stop the perversion. Edward Durall Stone, commissioned by the Department of Housing and Urban Development (HUD), published a study on modular housing that was flexible, stackable, doable, and doomed in a country where the only thing that matters is detached single-family residences.

By the eighties, most suburban developers were at least starting to mix and match a variety of floor plans and elevations (usually four of each) and occasionally turning houses towards the side yards and varying front setback depths in an effort to alleviate the oppressive visual boredom. Suburbia got a little better, which was unfortunately offset by the fact that it grew twice as large.

By the nineties, the high cost of housing finally outdistanced the lending capabilities of the VA, FHA, and HUD funding programs. It became painfully obvious that being middle class in America did not necessarily guarantee that you could own your own home. The overpriced inventory finally exceeded what the market could bear. Real estate agents who took to creative methods of financing were looked upon as messiahs to a working class who would do anything, even accept the bondage of a second mortgage, in order to own their own homes. Clearly, the inmates were running the asylum.

During this decade, mobile home builders increased their unit size, cleaned up their ticky-tacky image, and changed their name to Manufactured Housing. Quoting Delores Hayden again from *Redesigning the American Dream:*

> *Many manufacturers saw in the mobile home the legal and economic possibilities for cheap shelter, financed on the installment plan like an automobile and designed to standards lower than local building or zoning codes might have permitted for regular tract housing. The vagaries of the*

> *construction trades could be bypassed in the factory and so could some of the rules made by planning boards and mortgage bankers. Choice of styles expanded. The industry grew, until in 1999 an astonishing 20 percent of new single-family dwellings were mobile homes.* [9]

I live in a manufactured home. It has three bedrooms, two baths, and is 1,450 square feet in size. The exterior walls have 2x6 studs and beefed-up insulation, a thirty-pound snow load roof, and a complete appliance package. Yes, initially it looked like a manufactured home. The good news is that it cost $48,000. I couldn't touch this package with conventional construction methods. It would cost at least three times as much.

With $10,000 devoted to a landscape package, the exterior is now so well covered that you wouldn't know how it was built. And here is the truth about single-family housing of the future. *How the home is sited, and how the exterior amenity package (especially outdoor living areas) is arranged will have more to do with a comfortable lifestyle than any number of building facades.*

Manufactured housing could keep the middle class in this country in contact with the American dream, which is and always has been individual home ownership.

Complete site utilization with the home acting as an interior nucleus for weather protection and nighttime security will be the wave of the future.

Multifamily development, be it condominium, apartment, nursing home, or homeless shelter, is in need of theoretical and physical revamping. The most important element in this rejuvenation will be the treatment of open space, because wherever open space occurs, the opportunity exists for interfacing with nature and natural processes.

Housing in America, and worldwide for that matter, needs

to rise up within the immediate environment/habitat type rather than rolling over and eliminating it. Back to Ian McHarg and *Design with Nature,* the key word being *with.* Man and nature could exist at a level of environmental purity that, while perhaps not the optimum of being truly wild, could be several levels better than it currently is. Again, the objective is to be satisfied with our day-to-day surroundings, especially their natural aspects, so as to stop encroaching farther into rapidly dwindling habitat areas.

Heaven on Earth. People happy with the homes they're in. Inner-city neighborhoods stabilizing rather than being places to flee from if and when you acquire the means. Aspiration and ambition, while always looked upon as an inalienable right and a noble goal, can also serve to make us miserable. Our upward mobility to improve our lives and the lives of our offspring frequently leads to a downward spiral for the environment. Can mankind with its insatiable desire to acquire land on which to build houses truly exist in a quasi-symbiotic or live-and-let-live relationship with nature? No. Not unless we reduce our offspring and rethink our homes and, even more than that, identify what it is that would produce contentment in our lives. Nine times out of ten it's not your house. Not at all.

Saving the planet. What does it matter? Why bother? Mr. bin Laden and other zealots like him seem bent on death and destruction in the name of eternal salvation in some form of an afterlife. I wish they would get a life. What kind of God is it or what is their understanding of the will of their God that condones murder? Should their beliefs and actions prove to us that it is useless to try to protect the environment and thus save the planet? Not at all. If we reduce our efforts at environmental protection and/or restoration or just plain give up, then we are not subduing the Earth, we are letting it go to hell in some despot's handcart.

Genghis Kahn, Shaka Zulu, and Hitler, to name but a few, are dead and gone and so too will be bin Laden, either by our hand or Father Time's.

The Earth has endured wars so far, although even the most narrow-minded technician and scientist will admit the odds aren't very good for mankind in the event of a nuclear holocaust. But up until that time, and any sane man prays that it will never come, mankind is the steward of this green and blue and impossibly beautiful planet.

Genesis, the first book of the Bible, makes it pretty clear that God is God and since he made the world he can just as easily destroy it and call mankind into judgment. The last book of the Bible, the book of Revelation, while being exhaustively apocalyptic, is also quite unclear as to what becomes of the Earth. I've always been taught with Roman Catholic certainty that Christ will come from the sky with a shout, vanquish his enemies, and take his faithful following (living and dead) back up to Heaven with him. In Revelation, written by the apostle John, it isn't quite that simple:

> *Then I saw a new earth (with no oceans) and a new sky, for the present earth and sky had disappeared. And I, John, saw the Holy City, the new Jerusalem, coming down from God out of heaven. It was a glorious sight, beautiful as a bride at her wedding.*
>
> *I heard a loud shout from the throne saying, "Look, the home of God is now among men, and he will live with them and they will be his people; yes, God himself will be among them. He will wipe away all tears from their eyes, and there shall be no more death, nor sorrow, nor crying, nor pain. All of that has gone forever.*

Did he really mean that the present Earth would disappear or that God would rework it? The only thing that makes any sense to me at all is that God is to live among the faithful of mankind. And since He's coming down to rework the planet as opposed to taking me up (if I'm so fortunate) and out of this mess, then I want Him to know that I did everything I could to keep the Earth in reasonably good condition until he gets here.

I laugh when we humans talk about saving the planet because it seems so presumptuous. What we are really talking about is saving our asses. What have we done with our God-given gift of intelligence? No other species on Earth has devised a method by which to eradicate itself. No, we are quite alone in this endeavor. Webster's second definition of intelligence is my favorite. It says:

> *The capacity to meet situations, especially if new or unforeseen, by a rapid and effective adjustment of behavior . . .*

If only this were true, we would be well on our way to saving the planet.

Then the mighty angel standing on the sea and land lifted his right hand to heaven, and swore by him who lives forever and ever, who created heaven and everything in it and the earth and all that it contains and the sea and its inhabitants, that there should be no more delay, but that when the seventh angel blew his trumpet, then God's veiled plan—mysterious through the ages ever since it was announced by his servants the prophets—would be fulfilled . . . Then he told me, "You must prophesy further about many peoples, nations, tribes, and kings."

—Revelation 10:5–7, 10:11
The Living Bible